Lecture Notes in Computer Scie

Edited by G. Goos, J. Hartmanis, and J. van

Springer
Berlin
Heidelberg
New York
Barcelona
Hong Kong
London
Milan
Paris
Tokyo

Matthias Pflanz

On-line Error Detection and Fast Recover Techniques for Dependable Embedded Processors

Springer

Series Editors

Gerhard Goos, Karlsruhe University, Germany
Juris Hartmanis, Cornell University, NY, USA
Jan van Leeuwen, Utrecht University, The Netherlands

Matthias Pflanz
IBM Deutschland Entwicklung GmbH
Department of Processor Development II
Schönaicher Str. 220, 71032 Böblingen, Germany
E-mail: mpflanz@de.ibm.com

Cataloging-in-Publication Data applied for

Die Deutsche Bibliothek - CIP-Einheitsaufnahme

Pflanz, Matthias:
On-line error detection and fast recover techniques for dependable embedded
processors / Matthias Pflanz. - Berlin ; Heidelberg ; New York ; Barcelona ;
Hong Kong ; London ; Milan ; Paris ; Tokyo : Springer, 2002
  (Lecture notes in computer science ; Vol. 2270)
  ISBN 3-540-43318-X

CR Subject Classification (1998): C.1, C.3, C.4, B.6, B.8

ISSN 0302-9743
ISBN 3-540-43318-X Springer-Verlag Berlin Heidelberg New York

Springer-Verlag Berlin Heidelberg New York
a member of BertelsmannSpringer Science+Business Media GmbH

http://www.springer.de

© Springer-Verlag Berlin Heidelberg 2002
Printed in Germany

Typesetting: Camera-ready by author, data conversion by Olgun Computergrafik
Printed on acid-free paper   SPIN 10846131   06/3142   5 4 3 2 1 0

Preface

This thesis is a summary of my work as a research assistant in the Computer Engineering Research Group of the Computer Science Department at Brandenburg Technical University, Cottbus, Germany. It embraces the concepts, approaches, implementations, and experiments of my work on dependable processor-based embedded systems.

I would like to thank all those, who were directly or indirectly involved in the completion of this thesis, for their support.

Especially, I am grateful to my supervisor and mentor Prof. Dr. Heinrich-Theodor Vierhaus for the motivation regarding this interesting and versatile topic, for the excellent support of my work, for the permanent technical discussion, and for multitudinous ideas and suggestions.

I would like to thank my consultants Prof. Dr.-habil. M. Gössel from the University of Potsdam, Germany and Prof. Dr. Matteo Sonza Reorda from the Politecnico di Torino, Italy for their helpful remarks and hints.

My colleagues T. Mohaupt, O. Kluge, and U. Berger, I would like to thank for giving me the benefit of their experiences and critiques. I would like to acknowledge the support of our secretary, Kathleen Lück, with organizational and administrative tasks. Due to her assistence, many bureaucratic hurdles were removed.

A special thanks goes to the student members of our research group, Andreas Behling, Christian Galke, Falk Pompsch, Christian Rousselle, Thomas Schwanzara-Bennoit, and Karsten Walther, for their tireless co-operation during various investigations.

Finally, I would like to thank my wife Kathrin Pflanz for her infinite patience and support during the preparation of this thesis.

September 2001   Matthias Pflanz

Abstract

This thesis summarizes investigations and experiments on on-line observation and concurrent checking of processors. The objective was to detect single and/or multiple errors within one clock cycle.

First, refined techniques for data-path observation were investigated. Based on an approach for an observation of an ALU by Berger code prediction (BCP), the principle was extended to observe complete data-path structures to detect unidirectional errors.

The applicability of BCP to more complex data-paths with floating-point units was shown with the help of single and double-precision addition/subtraction floating-point-units. Therefore, prediction formulas were developed, which consider the operation in multi-stage units.

The cross-parity observation technique was developed especially for the on-line observation of large register-files or control-registers. By checking row, column, and diagonal-parities, single and multiple register errors can be detected. Cross-parity vectors have a potential diagnosis capability.

Due to the critical character of the processor control-logic, different techniques were developed and investigated to detect single or multiple control-signal errors within the clock-cycle of occurrence. As a simple alternative for a fault-secure controller, a duplicated control-logic was implemented. The identification of control-word differences can be used for error-weighting a subsequent control and, finally, for further recovery strategies. As a practical solution for small processors, a triplicated structure was investigated. With it, a fault-tolerant generation of control-signals to compensate transient errors until the first permanent error was possible. An application-driven reduction (ADR) of control-logic was proposed to decrease the overhead, especially for embedded systems with standard CISCs and a limited number of applications.

To detect control-signal errors, a new approach was taken by the processor state machine. To solve the problem with the complexity of state-spaces of common microprocessors, active control-signals were considered as a definitive representation of a current processor activity – the processor state. Access to all control-signals being assured and transitions being neglected, a combinatorial observation could be realized. Control-signals were encoded to a state-code, which represents the current (legal) state of the processor. With an access to control-signal conditions (instruction, time, flag-variables), a controller-independent generation (prediction) of the same code was realized. A comparison of both identifies an illegal state-code. To manage more complex state machines, an application-driven reduced state-encoder or a state-space partitioning was proposed. For pipeline structures, a partitioned observation of states was implemented as an example.

As a consequence of a successful error detection within the same clock cycle, fast recovery techniques of the processor state were investigated. Starting from the positive oriented assumption that an error has a transient character, a fast repetition (rollback) of erroneous cycle(s) can deliver correct results. Time-intervals of many thousands of cycles in classical roll-back techniques can not satisfy demands for safety-critical applications. Therefore, a shorter time (rollback distance) for recovery was implemented by micro-rollback strategies. Recent approaches to micro-rollback can recover the corresponding structure in case of a transient error. But this technique fails in the case of permanent errors. Therefore, a double-processor architecture was investigated. The master-trailer structure turns out to be a suitable solution for small processors. The trailer is delayed for one cycle. With this plus on-line checked master, a fast repair (2 cycles) of transient errors can be executed by a backup of all master-registers by their counterparts in the trailer. The advantage is the function-takeover (3 cycles) in the case of a permanent-error occurrence.

For pipeline processors, a further-developed rollback technique considers on one hand dynamical execution lengths for different stages, and on the other hand different error weightings. Therefore, a priority control was proposed to manage different rollback-actions (necessary rollback distances) for the recovery of the pipeline. Possible are one-cycle micro-rollback, a pipeline stage-rollback, and a macro-rollback by re-filling the whole pipeline. In the worst case (lost all stored return points), a program re-execution is realized.

Proposed on-line error detection and fast recovery techniques should be a supplement to other methods. In combination with other on-line observation principles, and/or with a combined hardware-software (self-)test, these techniques are used to fulfill a complete self-check scheme for an embedded processor. Strategies for a static or dynamic (micro-) rollback are a useful solution for processor errors due to transient faults of non-recurring characteristics. Then an executed program can be continued as quickly as the implemented structure allows.

The overall approach for efficient on-line checking and fast recovery techniques enhances processor availability and improves the dependability of an embedded system at very reasonable additional costs.

Zusammenfassung

In dieser Arbeit werden Entwürfe und Implementierungen vorgestellt, die eine on-line Fehler-Erkennung und -Behandlung in eingebetteten Prozessoren realisieren. Ziel war die Entwicklung von Techniken zur Detektion im selben Maschinenzyklus.

Zuerst werden verbesserte und weiterentwickelte Techniken zur Überwachung von Prozessor-Datenpfaden vorgestellt. Ausgehend von einem Verfahren zur Überwachung einer arithmetisch-logischen Einheit (ALU) durch Berger-Code Vorhersage (BCP) wurde das Prinzip dahingehend erweitert, dass eine Erkennung von unidirektionalen Fehlern im gesamten Daten-Pfad eines Prozessors möglich ist.

Die Anwendbarkeit der Berger-Code-Vorhersage auf komplexere Daten-Pfade mit Fließkomma-Arithmetik wurde mit Hilfe von Additions/Subtraktions-Einheiten mit einfacher und doppelter Genauigkeit gezeigt. Hierfür wurden spezielle Prediktionsformeln entwickelt, die die Operation dieser mehrstufigen Komponenten berücksichtigen.

Für die parallele Überwachung von größeren Register-Files oder von Kontroll-Registern wurde die Cross-Parity-(Kreuz-Paritäten-)Überwachungstechnik entwickelt. Durch den Check von Zeilen-, Spalten- und Diagonal-Parität können Einzel- und Mehrfachfehler in Registern aufgespürt werden. Die Cross-Parity-Technik besitzt weiterhin das Potential zur Fehlerdiagnose.

Auf Grund des kritischen Charakters einer Prozessor-Kontroll-Logik wurden verschiedene Techniken entwickelt und untersucht, die eine Erkennung von einfachen und mehrfachen Kontroll-Signal-Fehlern im selben Maschinen-Zyklus ermöglichen. Als eine einfache Variante einer fehlersicheren Auslegung der Kontrol-Logik wurde eine Verdopplung vorgenommen. Die Identifizierung von Kontroll-Wort-Differenzen konnte für eine Fehler-Gewichtung bzw. für eine Prioritäten-Steuerung und letztendlich für die Auswahl der Fehlerbehandlungsmaßnahme verwendet werden.
Als eine praktische Lösung für kleinere Prozessoren wurde eine verdreifachte Struktur untersucht. Damit wird die fehler-tolerante Generierung von Kontroll-Signalen bis hin zum ersten permanten Fehler möglich. Insbesondere für eingebettete Systeme mit Standard-CISC-Prozessoren mit einer begrenzten Anzahl von Anwendungen wurde ein Verfahren entwickelt, mit dem Kontroll-Logiken anwendungs-spezifisch reduziert werden könnten. Damit konnte der Overhead verringert werden.

Ein weiteres Verfahren behandelt die on-line Erkennung von Kontroll-Signal-Fehlern durch Überwachung der Prozssor-Zustandsmaschine. Um das Problem der Komplexität von Prozessor-Zustandsmaschinen zu umgehen, wurden aktuelle Kontroll-Signale als definitive Repräsentation der aktuellen Prozessor-Aktivität bzw. des aktuellen Prozessor-Zustandes betrachtet. Unter Voraussetzung der Zugriffsmöglichkeit auf alle Kontroll-Signale und der Vernachlässigung von

Transitionen wurde eine kombinatorische Überwachung realisiert. Kontroll-Signale wurden in ein Zustands-Codewort kodiert, der den momentanen (legalen) Zustand des Prozessors repräsentiert. Mit einem Zugriff auf die entsprechenden Kontroll-Signal-Bedingungen (Befehlscode, Zeit- und Flag-Variablen) wurde eine Kontroller-unabhängige Generierung (Vorhersage) des selben Codes realisiert. Ein Unterschied im Vergleich beider bedeutet die Erkennung eines illegalen Zustandscodes. Um komplexere Zustandsmaschinen beherrschen zu können, werden zum Einen anwendungsspezifisch reduzierte Zustandskodierer und zum Anderen eine Zustandsraum-Aufteilung vorgeschlagen. Exemplarisch zur Überwachung einer Pipeline-Struktur wurde eine aufgeteilte Zustandsraum-Überwachung implementiert.

Als eine Konsequenz der schnellen Fehlererkennung im selben Takt wurden schnelle Wiederherstellungstechniken untersucht. Ausgehend von einer positiv-orientierten Annahme, dass jeder aufgetretene Fehler transienter Natur ist, sollte eine schnelle Wiederholung (Rollback) des fehlerhaften Zyklus korrekte Daten liefern. Zeitintervalle von mehreren tausend Zyklen in klassischen Rollback-Verfahren sind entsprechend der Anforderungen von sicherheits-kritischen Systemen ungeeignet. Deswegen wurde eine kürzere Rollback-Distanz mit Hilfe der Micro-Rollback-Strategie implementiert. Bisherige Rollback-Verfahren sind auf die Behandlung von transienten Fehlern ausgerichtet, versagen jedoch bei permanenten Fehlern. Hierfür wurde eine Doppel-Prozessor-Struktur untersucht. Die Master-Trailer-Architektur stellte sich dabei als exzellente Lösung für kleinere Prozessoren heraus. Ein Trailer ist gegenüber dem Master um einen Takt in der Programm-Abarbeitung verzögert. Damit und mit einer on-line Fehlererkennung kann eine schnelle (2 Zyklen) Reparatur ausgeführt werden, indem alle Master-Register mit den entsprechenden Trailer-Registern überschrieben werden. Der Vorteil besteht aber in der Möglichkeit der vollständigen Funktionsübernahme innerhalb von 3 Zyklen im Falle eines permanenten Fehlers im Master.

Für Pipeline-Prozessoren wurde die Rollback-Technik verfeinert und weiter-entwickelt. Zum Einen mußte eine dynamische Befehlsausführungslänge in unterschiedlichen Pipeline-Stufen und zum Anderen eine differenzierte Fehler-gewichtung berücksichtigt werden. Deswegen wurde eine Prioritäten-Steuerung entwickelt, die verschiedene Rollback-Aktionen mit unterschiedlichen Rollback-Distanzen steuert. Möglich sind Ein-Zyklus-Micro-Rollback, Pipeline-Stufenrollback und ein Macro-Rollback, bei dem die gesamte Pipeline neu gefüllt wird. Für den Fall, daß alle Rückkehrpunkte verloren bzw. fehlerhaft sind, wird eine Programm-Wiederholung ausgeführt.

Die vorgestellten on-line Fehlererkennungs- und -Behandlungs-Techniken sollen eine Ergänzung zu anderen Methoden darstellen. In Kombination mit anderen on-line Observierungstechniken und/oder mit einem kombinierten Hardware/Software-(Selbst-) Test können diese Techniken genutzt werden, um einen eingebetteten Prozessor vollständig selbst-überprüfend auszulegen. Strategien für ein statisches oder dynamisches (Micro-) Rollback sind nützliche Maßnahmen, um durch transiente Effekte verursachte Prozessor-Fehler auf effektive Art und Weise zu beheben. Ein ausgeführtes Programm kann so schnell fortgesetzt werden. Die vorgestellten Methoden verbessern die Verfügbarkeit eines eingebetteten Prozessors und damit auch dessen Zuverlässigkeit bei gleichzeitig moderaten zusätzlichen Kosten.

Contents

1. Introduction

1.1 Background and Motivation

Nowadays a great part of computing components is found in embedded systems for control and signal processing applications. The trend of embedded computer designs is moving towards single-chip solutions. So called systems-on-chip (SOCs) include various reusable functional blocks such as microprocessors, DSPs, accelerators, memories, and interfaces (embedded cores). The complexity of such systems causes a lot of new problems for developers and users. During the last 15 years, CMOS scaling offered new opportunities to system architects because of increasing frequency, transistor density and die size. On the other hand, the work of test engineers has become more complicated.

The integration of various cores on one chip hinders test by traditional methods because of inadequate accessibility to partial components. The probability of design and manufacturing defects not detected during IC production test grows with higher complexity. Additional influences and aging effects may cause system failure. Devices become more susceptible to transient faults due to increasing clock frequency and lower voltage swings between logic levels.

In embedded systems, various processor architectures are used to execute controlling or data-processing tasks. Consumer electronics, mobile communication, and multimedia systems such as computer games are the largest markets for such systems. But current embedded processor-based systems or SOCs also grow into application with a safety-critical relevance. A growing part of embedded processors are exposed to noisy environments like cars, public transportation systems, industrial processes, etc. Here, methodologies for validation, test or in the field observation gain a new significance. Traditional test and validation methods have to be adopted for a high error or fault coverage throughout the design process and after production. Methods for test and validation can be allocated to different fields of design and test technology [1]: e.g. design verification, component-level- or system-level-test, external- or self-test, off-line or on-line testing and many more. Test of systems in the field of application is gaining attention. Here we can distinguish between off-line tests, e.g. during a system start-up, and on-line tests during system operation. While off-line tests serve to detect permanent fault effects, on-line checks are necessary to detect transient fault effects, e.g. caused by crosstalk, glitches, delays or oscillations [2]. This aspect gains more and more importance in safety critical and/or real-time applications. The missing time-windows to process and to analyze test patterns make special methods for on-line detection of transient faults necessary. A lot of on-line test techniques have been developed in recent years. Previous developments resulted in add-on units like watchdog circuits for embedded systems with more or less overhead depending on the target system. Unfortunately, many investigation have only an academic character because manufacturers shun the overhead. Only unavoidable redundant hardware/software in systems with a demand for fault-tolerance is accepted. While a triple-modular redundancy (TMR) is the standard e.g. for avionics, it is too expensive for automotive control. Watchdog circuits have found large-scale applications in automotive systems. However, their capabilities are limited to the detection of large-scale system errors within a time frame of several up to hundreds of clock cycles. Repair actions are limited to system re-start operations. Detection and compensation of transient faults within a few clock cycles is far beyond their scope, left alone the correction of permanent faults.

Objectives of the research to be described in this thesis were to develop, to implement and to validate new techniques for on-line detection of permanent and transient faults of embedded processors. Such techniques should be tailored to application during the design process of application-specific processors or for the extension of 'open' processor cores.

Microprocessors are traditionally partitioned into a data-path (DP) and a control-path (CP). Observation would therefore also be partitioned into checks of data operation – respective data processing units, and control-flow – respective controller units. Because of the not insignificant amount of faults in real embedded systems caused by non-recurred effects, a distinction between permanent and transient faults as well as different fault handling strategies are necessary. A fast fault handling was a partial objective in case of transient effects to restore or backup processor state. On top of such capabilities, new processor schemes should include basic fault-secure characteristics in case of permanent faults.

An important point of the work was the investigation of various strategies to decrease the according hardware overhead for on-line test and backup-functionality. For solving these problems, the developed techniques are basically founded on two strategies, *ADR (application-driven reduction)* and *ASP (architecture-specific partitioning)*.

This thesis is partitioned into five chapters. The first chapter outlines the background and describes the motivation for on-line fault detection and fast correction in embedded microprocessors. This chapter introduces terminologies. Furthermore, a short overview is given about publications in context with results from the work in this thesis.

Chapter 2 outlines fault models according to characteristics such as 'permanent' and 'transient'. With a short introduction into processor history, the point of view of common processor architecture is explained. An illustration of the possible fault/error behavior of processors or processor components pursues the explanations according to the imperative necessity of error-detection and handling techniques. The chapter presents examples for errors in microprocessor control-path (CP) and data-path (DP).

On-line check strategies are distinguished to detect errors in components on one hand and to detect control signal errors on the other hand. Chapter 3 outlines the state-of-the-art error detection mechanisms – respective microprocessor component observation. Furthermore, methodologies are introduced which are derived from *Berger-code prediction* and *Cross-parity observation*.

Chapter 4 starts with an outline of recent research activities in the observation of controller errors. Then, two on-line observation techniques for control signals are presented. The *application-driven reduction* (ADR) principle to generate the so called *pseudo-TMR control logic* is introduced. A further technique is based on processor state-code or *control signal prediction (CSP)*.

Chapter 5 addresses the use of on-line check methodologies for the distinction between classes of permanent versus transient faults. This implies different fault handling strategies. A strategy for a processor *micro-rollback* for sequential and pipelined microprocessors is introduced and validated with the help of demonstration processor designs.

As a summary of concepts and implementations developed within the scope of this research project, chapter 6 discusses proposed schemes with regards to advantages and disadvantages. Furthermore, possibilities are explained to improve characteristics of proposed structures. Current and future work on this topic will be outlined.

Appendix contains further information according to implementations in preceding sections. For instance, the architectures of proprietary processor cores used as examples are described in more detail.

1.2 Terminology

1.2.1 Embedded Systems

An embedded system is a computer-based component or component group inside a mechanical, electrical or optical system. Main functions of this intelligent core are to control the system functionality and to process data. The basic structure is shown in Fig. 1. An embedded system may include interfaces, analog/digital converters, mixed-signal components, memory, user defined logic (UDL) and one or more processing units. (One is common for low-end systems and may be a single micro-controller or a digital signal processor (DSP).) For this component, the term *embedded processor* is used in this thesis. Some authors specify "embedded systems" to *embedded processor-based systems*. A single micro-controller can be seen as a minimum-size embedded systems.

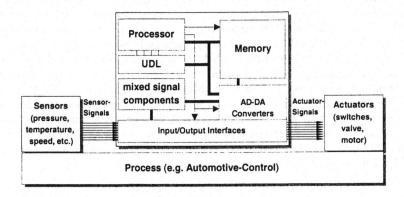

Fig. 1. Embedded systems - basic structure

Application fields for embedded systems are all kinds of controlling or data processing devices that run on a set of fixed software.

The set of distinct differences in comparison with general-purpose computing instructions such as PCs is as follows:

- specifically tailored to fit the application
- embedded software known in advance (often used without modification for the lifetime of the system)
- types of data known in most cases
- often real-time critical
- often safety-critical
- often extremely cost-sensitive
- often harsh environment
- life time dependent on host system
- often limited access for repair / maintenance

Fast temperature changes, vibrations and electromagnetic influences are common. Embedded systems in safety-critical applications such as airbag or brake control in cars must satisfy strongest demands for fault-tolerant software and hardware. The software should be able to handle every possible system state under normal and exceptional conditions, and the hardware must be designed for long-term, error-free operation. A reliable embedded system includes self-checks and self-diagnosis to localize faults or defects and to identify faulty components. Some systems even include on-line fault detection and mechanisms for error correction.

1.2.2 Cores

A core – respective an integrated circuit core – is a pre-designed building block for integrated circuits and systems that may replace a standard chip or IC with the same functionality. The core can be used together with other cores and user-defined logic in building a larger or more complex application on one chip. The current trend in system development is oriented towards integration of complete (earlier board-) system on one chip (SOC). The integrated circuit core is commonly a pre-verified building block given as a layout-level data base or a synthesiziable hardware description language (HDL). Types of cores can be divided into soft, firm or hard [3]. A *soft core* consists of a HDL-description that is often a structural or a RTL (register transfer level) description. The core user is able to change the design. A *firm core* is commonly a gate-level netlist that is ready for technology-dependent physical IC design. A *hard core* is often the layout with technology-dependent timing information. The core vendor delivers complete information for the chip developer (e.g. timing specifications and test patterns). Firm and hard cores are unchangeable by the core user because of hidden functional / structural information.

Cores include design know-how, and they are subject to patents or copy-rights. A core block represents an intellectual property (IP) that the core vendor licenses to a core user. Core vendors and semiconductor manufacturers have built the organization RAPID (Reusable Application Specific Intellectual Property Developers) to control the distribution and to protect the copy-rights.

Examples of integrated circuit cores are microprocessors, DSPs, hardware accelerators for common algorithms, interface controllers, memories and so on.

Because the design and the use of cores have to go by rules, core vendors have founded the Virtual Socket Interface Alliance (VSIA: http://www.vsi.org). Their goal is a core specification which is independent from vendor and from target technology. This specification should allow a high portability and the reusability ("Mix and Match" similar to "Plug and Play").

In this work the term *core* is used exclusively for the category *soft core*. Developed processors are designed as RTL-schematics and structural VHDL–(VHSIC Hardware Description Language; VHSIC...Very High Speed Integrated Circuit)–descriptions.

1.2.3 System-on-Chip

The focus of digital system design has changed from system-on-board (SOB) to the embedded core-based system-on-chip (SOC). A SOC may include various reusable functional blocks (cores) such as microprocessors, memories, DSP, bus controllers and interfaces. Fig. 2 shows the structure of a potential SOC.

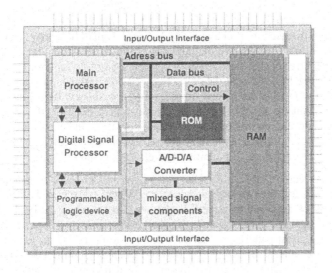

Fig. 2. A possible SOC scheme

In comparison to a system on a board (SOB), there exist similarities but the most critical challenge for the development of SOCs is the test after production [4], [5]. For the SOB approach, the IC design, manufacturing and testing are all done by the IC manufacturer. Therefore, the system integrator can assume fault-free ICs. The integrator has to test only the interconnects between the ICs. A well known technique to address this test problem is the Boundary Scan Test or JTAG [Joint Test Action Group] or the IEEE 1149.1 standard [6]. For the manufacturing of a SOC, the provider delivers only a *description* of the core. It is impossible to test his core for manufacturing defects before actual system integration. Essentially, the responsibility for the test of embedded processors shifts from the processor vendor to the system integrator. Most likely, the core-user is not a processor company and does not have equipment for processor test available. On the top of the complexity problem associated with SOCs, this is a second potential pit-fall.

The IEEE P1500 Working Group has been working towards a standardization of the test (test interfaces, languages, architecture constraints) for embedded cores [7].

Beyond the manufacturing test, the 'in-field' on-line observation of SOCs is a problem. Solutions have been proposed such as Built-in Self-test (BIST), modified to serve SOCs. Other solutions are given with the migration of traditional and new test techniques implemented in software to run on an on-chip test controller [8] or the use of existing components (processors, scan-chains) for test [9].

1.2.4 Test and Check

Fundamental terms in the test or check of integrated circuit design are *fault, error* and *failure*. Definitions are given in [10] which was basically derived from a dictionary: A *fault* is a blemish, weakness or shortcoming of a particular hardware or software component. Examples are e.g. a physical defect in semiconductor structure of chip layout, external influenced misbehavior of electrical signal flow. An *error* is the manifestation of a fault – respective the deviation from correct behavior of hardware or software. If the error causes the system to perform one of its functions incorrectly, then a system *failure* has occurred (see also Fig. 16). For instance, a transistor in an arithmetic logic unit (ALU) has a permanent fault (e.g. a short with ground or stuck-at-0). Due to this fault the result of an operation may be erroneous. If the result of this operation was an address, for instance for a branch operation, the error may result in a system failure because of a wrong memory access. A distinction between fault classes according to their characteristics in duration and effect is given in chapter 5.

To validate the correctness of an electronic design, various kinds of tests can be executed. A system *test* is an experiment in which the system is exercised and its resulting responses will be analyzed to ascertain whether it behaved correctly [1]. In order to test a digital system for faults, specific function and/or structure dependent and often highly optimized test patterns are used for stimulation [11]. With the help of pre-calculated response patterns, it is possible to draw conclusions on faults or fault locations. In this work the main objective is the embedded processor. A test of a whole processor with random patterns or pattern sequences is difficult at best. The first reason is the sequential depth of processor designs. Common handling routines for unknown op-codes, exceptions and interrupts forbid the execution of 'random machine-code'. A processor simulation can be seen as a functional test with a small set of deterministic patterns.

Test strategies can be organized along different levels of abstraction from the design process (e.g. transistor-, logic-level, RTL, instruction set level, processor-, system-level). Costs for the test of complex embedded systems decrease if it is executed at higher levels. A test at RT- or behavioral level is in most cases shorter and less costly than a switch-level test. For example, switch level test for faults on transistors and interconnects (stuck-on/off, line bridge/break) is about 10 time more costly in ATPG (automatic test pattern generation) effort and test set size than a gate-level stuck-at test (for static CMOS logic). The test at a higher level cannot reliably cover faults at deeper levels, or with a high level test strategy it may be impossible to model low level faults. A good solution is mixed-level fault simulation and test generation [12], [13], [14]. Test methods can also be divided according to timing (offline or on-line) and stimuli-source criterions (external- or self-test). The pattern sets used for digital IC testing are often generated from structural information, or they are of a pseudo-random nature (as in built-in self-test – BIST). In the second case, they show little correlation with the real control or data flow of a processor. In this work the term *check* is used for the observation of a real data throughput or real control sequences whereby the processor is an active and clocked device. Examples for check procedures are to analyze an encoded result, the comparison of result of duplicated components, the comparison with a predicted result and so on (see also chapter 3 and 4).

1.2.5 Fault-Tolerance Objectives

Fault-Tolerance (FT) is the property of a system to continue defined functions or tasks after and in spite of the occurrence of faults. The goal of FT is to prevent system failure from occurring [10]. FT techniques are based on redundancy. An overview is given in Table 1.

Table 1. FT Techniques

Hardware redundancy	Concurrent (possible diverse) operating hardware components (duplication, triplication, etc.)
Software redundancy	Diverse developed SW with the same functionality;
Data redundancy	Data coding (Cyclic codes, Parity, Berger code, etc.)
Time redundancy	Multiple calculation of same data; Time windows in operation flow for test or check;
Functional redundancy	Functional similarity of sub-circuits; Emulation of HW-functionality with software
Hybrid redundancy	Combination of different techniques;

A typical fault-tolerant processor scheme is the triple-modular redundant (TMR) structure shown in Fig. 3.

Processors execute an application concurrently. Results are compared through a voting circuit. In case of the occurrence of a fault in one processor (respective in case of result-differences), it reaches a majority decision trough a two out of three majority voting. Because of the improbability of two equal faults in two processors, the voting principle guarantees a decision for the right result. Furthermore, designers of ft systems tend to implement three processors in a divers manner with respect to hardware and software. Then TMR can handle transient faults, permanent hardware faults and even hardware/software design errors, only specification errors may escape. Such structures are FT with respect to the first permanent fault in one processor. After a permanent fault in one processor, the system works *fault-secure* because a fault is then only detectable from the comparison of two processors.

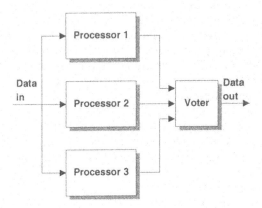

Fig. 3. TMR-Processor scheme

A FT-system must not necessarily be based on schemes with multiple processors (2-of-3, 3-of-5, etc.) Redundant components at a finer granularity, self-checking and error correcting facilities, and multiple operation with the same data make a system fault-tolerant. Chapter 3 explains state-of-the-art in this topic and proposes new fault-tolerant structures.

The system *dependability* summarizes the concepts of reliability, availability, and safety [10]. The *reliability* of a system is characterized trough the conditional probability that within a time interval the system performs correctly. The system *availability* is defined as the conditional probability of a correct function at an instant of time. *Safety* is the probability that a system will either continue its function correctly or will degrade its performance or will discontinue the functions in the manner that causes no harm. The characteristic 'safety' is demanded for systems whose failure can harm people, animals or material resources.

1.2.6 Safety-Critical Embedded Systems

In recent years, embedded systems experienced a widespread use in various industrial areas. Starting from automation of complicated controlling mechanism like automatic brake control, avionics, etc., embedded systems find application-fields also in consumer electronics and mobile communication or computer peripherals.

If a misbehavior or a failure of such systems can harm life and health of human beings, it is *safety-critically*. Embedded systems with this special characteristic are e.g. controllers in transportation systems or in nuclear reactors.

Often harsh environment conditions such as fast temperature changes, mechanical vibrations, and electromagnetic radiation influence components and may cause harm to the function of safety-critical embedded systems. An aggravating circumstance is also given with a long-term application because the system behavior e.g. after 10 years of operation including wear-out is difficult to simulate and so rarely predictable. An example for a long-term safety-critical embedded system is the automatic brake control in a car. Systems in cars are designed to function for 10 years or 100.000 km and may have to do so much longer without ever being serviced. Autonomous systems like space probes are also long-term systems with a safety-critical relevance. Missing (because impossible) service intervals should not influence the primary function.

In order to fulfill demands of safety-critical embedded systems, hardware and software engineers developed many approaches and techniques. The objective of this thesis is a contribution to increase the dependability of embedded processors at reasonable level of extra cost.

1.3 Publications

During the work on this thesis, ideas, implementations, and experiences were proposed in various publications. This section gives a short overview about contents of published papers and explains novelty of approaches, which will be described in more detail in further chapters of this thesis.

In "Generating Reliable Embedded Processors" [15] a new concept for the design of fault-tolerant embedded processors – focussed on control logic – was proposed. Fault-tolerant systems rely on various redundancy strategies. For an enormous number of safety-critical applications, the overhead for additional hardware (e.g. TMR) is unacceptable, especially for automotive controllers. We introduced a more efficient solution for redundant hardware. It bases on an application-driven reduction (ADR) principle.

Here a special feature of embedded processors was exploited: General purpose processors with a large instruction set are often implemented in an embedded system, which executes one or a small number of programs. Embedded applications need in most cases only a small subset of the complete instruction set. The idea was here the analysis of given application or machine code and re-generation of a reduced control-logic. The smaller blocks were implemented together with the original one. With this, a so-called pseudo-TMR was realized, which has the same characteristics as a regular TMR for the present application, but at a lower overhead level. Furthermore, it was proposed to carry out ADR also for other components of an embedded processor or to exclude unused components.

The paper "Possibilities and Limitations of Self-Test and Functional Backup for Standard Processor Cores in Embedded Applications" [16] described investigations on modified redundancy with the help of programmable devices. An implementation of regular hardware plus programmable logic in three variants was proposed. The potential of programmable logic devices was investigated in order to replace erroneous processor components – respective to perform a self-repair. Interconnect delays in multi-chip solutions are a significant limitation. The needed gate count for processor cores is often a bottleneck for low-price PLDs. Furthermore, long re-programming times are not useful for a fast repair or for real-time constraints. An advantage is the ability to update test or backup features.

New generations of PLDs or FPGAs offer higher performance and excellent features, so that a combined use with hardwired logic is more promising. In today's embedded systems, some variants of hardwired logic plus programmable devices or arrays are used (e.g. Infineon's Tricore^{TM})

Various possibilities to detect transient and permanent faults during the operation were investigated in "An Efficient On-line–Test and Recover Scheme for Embedded Processors" [17]. The goal was a high grade of dependability for such systems. We proposed different ideas to detect errors on-line. Data-path components are observed by Berger code check. To observe control signals, the control-signal prediction technique was introduced. To distinguish between a transient or a permanent character of faults, a comparison of a stored fault vector (first wrong program-part) and the actual fault (further fault after program-part repetition) and was proposed .

In "Efficient Backup Schemes for Processors in Embedded Systems" [18] we presented schemes for embedded processors which target a long-term dependability by handling even a series of transient faults in an efficient way. It is based on online recognition and repair of non-permanent faults using a self-checkable pseudo-TMR processor scheme or a processor roll-back strategy. For faults that are recognized as permanent, possibilities and limitations of reconfiguration or self-repair by using (in-field-) programmable logic devices were discussed. To increase the efficiency of a dependable embedded processor structure, the ADR-strategy for additional test and backup components was used.

The approach "An Efficient On-line Test and Back-up Scheme for Embedded Processors" [19] duplicates only the truly necessary parts of a standard processors for test and back-up purposes including capabilities of on-line self test. Transient faults are recognized and compensated. In a second step, the back-up processor itself becomes fully self-testing and fault tolerant towards a highly dependable system solution by state-encoding of control paths and an Berger code check in the data path.

To handle or to repair a detected error, an improved micro-rollback technique was introduced. Here a fault within the operation of a processor is assumed first as a transient effect, then a repetition of erroneous cycle seems to be the easiest solution. Against classical rollback techniques with a long roll-back distance – respective with a long repetition time, a micro-rollback with repetition of exactly one cycle was proposed. This technique was realized with a (reduced) trailer-processor, which executes the same code but with a delay of one cycle. An error caused by a transient effect can be handled by re-writing of all registers of the master processor by the contents of trailer registers. The trailer processor is able to take over the whole function in case of a permanent error within the master processor. To handle a transient faults, a delay of two cycles was reached. If a permanent fault occurs, the processor function is continued after three cycles.

The principle of on-line observation of processor control-flow graphs was presented in "A New Method for On-line State Machine Observation for Embedded Microprocessors" [20]. In this paper we propose an efficient method to observe a processor state machine and to detect illegal states within one clock-cycle. The strategy is based on a comparison of an encoded vector VCP1, representing the real state, and a predicted vector VCP2, representing the expected state.

In order to allow a use of processor state-encoding technique also for control-signal on-line check in more complex processors (especial for processors with a pipelined or super-scalar operation), a state-machine partitioning was introduced.

To minimize the overhead, we investigated different strategies to modify check units. A reduction of hardware overhead can be reached by application-specific reduction of processor state machines.

The paper "On-line Error Detection Techniques for Dependable Embedded Processors with High Complexity" [21] proposed new on-line error detection techniques in data path structures. It deals with concurrent check methods for complex data-path elements like FPUs or register-files. A Berger code prediction unit for a multistage add-sub-FPU is proposed. Furthermore, the suitability of Berger code for register-files is discussed. As an alternative, the Cross-Parity observation is introduced. Cross-Parity bases on the calculation of three parity vectors of a register-file: the (commonly used) row parity, the column parity and the diagonal parity. The observation is realized with a comparison of the real and the predicted Cross-Parity. The Cross-Parity technique is registered for a patent.

2. Fault Models and Fault-Behavior of Processor Structures

During the process of specification, design and implementation of an embedded system, various types of faults are possible. Fig. 4 outlines the according fault parts during the whole development process:

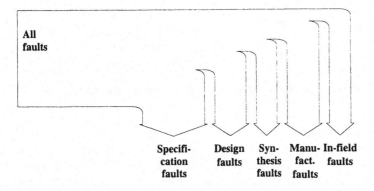

All faults

Specifi- cation faults   **Design faults**   **Syn- thesis faults**   **Manu- fact. faults**   **In-field faults**

Fig. 4. Fault Parts during System Development

In this thesis, specification or design faults are not addressed. Faults which arise from the manufacturing process can be classified as follows: **Signal line faults** can be *break* (a signal line or a contact is interrupted) or *bridge* (Signal lines are unintentionally connected). A strong short of a signal line with GND (stuck-at-0), with VDD (stuck-at-1) or with another signal line (line bridge) is a 'hard' bridge fault – respective a permanent fault. On the other hand, a high-impedance bridge or a pinhole connection between lines may cause a dynamic fault, e.g. by an increased gate- or path-delay. These effects can be assigned to parametric faults. **Transistor faults** are often caused by parametric faults. In MOS (Metal-Oxide-Semiconductor) transistor circuits, the silicon oxide is used as an insulation material and as the gate oxide. Therefore, *oxide faults* are a common reason for transistor failures. If the gate oxide is too thin, for instance, the transistor is susceptible to permanent gate damage by voltage peaks. Also, material pollution is possible. Here, mobile ions can exist under high-voltage condition which may be accumulated near the gate and cause a shift of the transistor threshold voltage.

A further class are *metal defects*, e.g. line breaks, metal over-alloying and migration of metal ions. *Surface defects* are caused by pollution of the crystal surface during the manufacturing process. Due to this effect, mobile ions emerge at the chip surface which are the reason for additional charge carriers, parasitic transistors or faulty current paths. Inadequate etching or chemical remains may cause corrosion effects, which may reduce the thickness of aluminum signal lines, or they may cause shorts e.g. between signal and power-lines. Examples are shown in Figure 5 and 6.

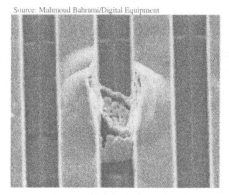

Fig. 5. A Layer-remain after etching   **Fig. 6. A Short after inadequate etching**

Production test techniques is a well investigated research area and can cover most of the manufacturing faults. However, any defect that causes neither significant parameter shifts (quiescent power, input supply current, power dissipation) nor measurable functional effects will escape its detection by production tests. Such defects may eventually trigger functional faults after stress or further corrosion. In [22] the "bathtub curve" describes the failure rate of an electronic system during its lifetime. For instance, hidden defects may cause failures early in lifetime – the so called "infant mortality". After a *steady state* the system has a relative constant failure rate (dependent on the according quality). In the *wear-out phase*, the failure rate increases again because of aging effects. These effects may be due to 'slight' manufacturing faults which grow up into defects. The *electromigration* is an example for formation of defects on power-lines within an IC [23]. Due to a permanent mono-directional current, moving metal-ions cause voids and hillocks (see also Fig. 7). Line with voids can break like a fuse or hillocks may grow to shorts with other lines or can influence semiconductor structures.

Another problem will gain importance to avoid in-field failures – single-event upsets [24] caused by cosmic radiation. This radiation with up to 20 neutrons per cm² and an energy level greater than 10 MeV causes no harm to today's integrated circuits. But a dependable function will be imperiled with shrinking geometries below 0,1 μm or voltage level less than 2.2 V. Nicolaidis forecasts that random error rates by these influences will become unacceptable in the next few years [25]. Therefore, on-line techniques for error detection and fast recovery is likely to gain more and more importance not only for safety-critical application, but also to avoid obstruction of the technological progress.

Source: IEEE Spectrum, Sept. 96, p. 75

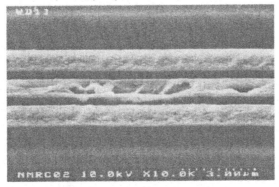

Fig. 7. Effects of Electromigration in IC-powerlines

2.1 Fault Models

2.1.1 Permanent Faults

All defects or effects can be classified as sources of permanent faults if their occurrence causes a reproducible error. Sources of permanent faults are real physical defects caused by manufacturing faults, pollution or material weaknesses. A classical model for such faults is the *single-stuck* model. It was the first most widely studied model [1]. This model represents different physical faults, and it can be used to model other types of faults. Experiences have shown that a test for single-stuck may detect also many other non-classical faults [1]. It is independent from technology. The number of faults that need an explicit test can be reduced by fault-collapsing techniques. An approach to collapse list for temporary faults is described in [26].

Fault models were first introduced by Eldred in the late 1950s [27]. Since then, the models *stuck-at-zero* (sa0) and *stuck-at-one* (sa1) have been the main base of test technology, despite a number of shortcomings. For production test, often a single stuck-at (ssa) fault model is assumed. The sa0 model represents a permanent connection of gate inputs or the output with ground or Vss. Respectively the sa1 is a model for a junction with logic cell power supply line or Vdd. Figure 8 shows examples for sa0 and sa1 faults on in- and on outputs of a NAND-gate. Stuck-at faults can be simulated at the transistor-, at the gate and at the RTL (saX at macro-in- and outputs).

Other models for permanent faults include *stuck-open* or *stuck-close* models, which represent a permanent open respective close transistor [28]. Figure 9 shows examples for these faults in a NAND-cell. If we assume all transistors of the CMOS circuit as enhancement types – the pMOS transistor MP1 has a stuck-open and the transistor MN1 has a stuck-close fault because of permanent junction of the gate with Vdd. Stuck-close faults in CMOS circuits may be detected by IDDQ-monitoring [29].

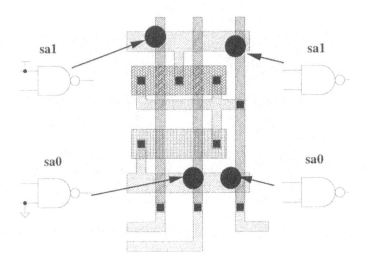

Fig. 8. Stuck-at-0/1 on NAND In-and Outputs

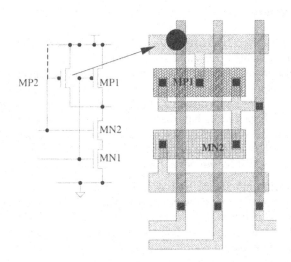

Fig. 9. Stuck-open and Stuck-close Fault

A disadvantage of this model is that it can only be simulated explicitly at the switch- or the transistor level. At higher level the stuck-at models becomes more expedient.

For the described models above, ideal shorts were assumed. Other models which represent physical defects are *bridging faults* [30], [31], [32]. The behavior of semiconductor structures may be changed if a bridge or a junction has a resistance value in the kΩ-range. A bridge may cause transistor stuck-close behavior fault due to a low-resistance bridge between source and drain. A bridging fault between input and output of a gate is determined by the relative impedance condition in the input-driving stage and the relative value of the resistor [33].

Another possibility for permanent faults is the occurrence of dynamical effects like *path delays*. This effect may also depend on the resistance value of a line bridge. A low-resistance causes often a delay or even a stuck-fault. But a high-resistance bridge may cause negligible delays or exceptionally even a speed-up of signals [33]. Most permanent faults can be detected with test patterns or by redundancy techniques [10] outlined in table 1.

2.1.2 Transient Faults

In semiconductor companies, test costs contribute a large fraction of the entire IC design- and production costs. This test contains mostly the test for permanent faults or defects from manufacturing process. Beyond permanent faults, integrated systems of recent years are more susceptible to temporary effects like *transient* and *intermittent* faults. They are the major portion of digital system malfunctions, and have been found to account for more than 90% of the total maintenance expense [34]. But it is impossible to reproduce or to simulate all effects in advance that may occur during the lifetime on an embedded system. These effects may be electromagnetic influences, single-event upset through alpha-particle radiation, power supply fluctuation or even 'soft' faults. The errors as a result of these faults are troublesome due to their potential for a system failure, and elude many current testing methods. New faults emerge during the system life time or due to changed operation parameters. Intermittent faults can occur due to partially defective components, loose connections. Especially 'weak' faults contain the risk of an error if they grow up to breaks or bridges. Examples are given in Fig. 10 and can also be assigned to Fig. 5-7.

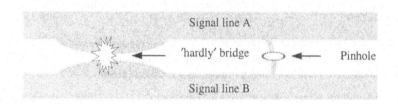

Fig. 10. Weak Faults Between Signal Lines

In poor designs a too small distance between lines (hardly bridge) injures defined layout rules. It may caused steady, but not regular recurred voltage breaks through the isolation material. Some faults have the characteristic to heal during the life time. An example is a weak short or a pinhole. It can be assigned to high-resistance bridges. It may be blown like a fuse if a voltage difference between lines is exceeded. A further hardly testable fault is a bridge fault with a feedback effect. For instance, a bridge between input and output causes different erroneous behavior [11]

Further transient faults are crosstalk or glitches. An example for effects of signal coupling at two lines is outlined in Fig. 11. It shows possible signal distortions at one line in the case of a signal change at the other line.

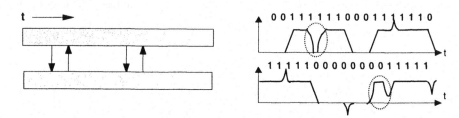

Fig. 11. Possible Signal Line Crosstalk Effects

The fault model *bit-flip* represents the flipping of a signal value at signal lines, within register or memory cells . The bit-flip model may be structured into the model *flip-to-1* (ft1) and *flip-to-0* (ft0). The distortion in the signal value (encircled) in the upper time diagram in Fig. 11 shows the effect of a ft0 fault. A ft1 is outlined in the lower diagram.

The *delay* model is a further model also for transient effects. Beyond recurrent path or gate delays (permanent delay) because of inadequate timing simulation, this effect can be caused by external influences or changing material characteristics. A delay has particularly an effect in write or store operations in embedded processors (e.g. rising edge at the register clock and delayed data or delayed enable signal).

Transient faults may be classified into following groups according to fault injection experiments [35]:

1. **Effective** errors corrupt control and/or data flow with or without latency.
2. **Overwritten** errors have no effect on any further operation.
3. Errors that have no effect during operation are called **latent**.

In the fault simulation environment HEARTLESS [36], [37], [38] that has the capability for fault injection, we did not take ineffective errors into account. Examples are data line bit-flips to a register outside a writing process (e.g. enable/load = false). Faults which cause overwritten errors are removed from fault lists within the fault collapsing process.

In [10], a transient fault detection with a repetition of computations is proposed. Essentially, this implies a triple execution of states, storage of results and comparison. Therefore and because of the off-line non-testability of explained effects, an on-line detection is strongly necessary to handle errors in the fastest way in order to avoid system failure.

2.2 Embedded Processor Architectures

2.2.1 Control and Data Path

For later comments in following chapters, this section explains the general view of the basic processor structure.

Processors can generally be classified into the 'von Neumann'- and the 'Harvard'-Architecture [39]. From 1936 to 1938, Konrad Zuse developed and built the first binary digital computer of the world (Zl). The first fully functional program-controlled electromechanical digital computer in the world (the Z3) was completed by Zuse in 1941, but was destroyed in 1944 during the World War II [40]. A copy was made in 1960 and put on display in the German Museum ("Deutsches Museum") in Munich. American authors have claimed for decades that the first operational electronic, general-purpose computers was built by J. Presper Eckert and John Mauchly in their ENIAC (Electronic Numerical Integrator and Calculator) during the war and was published in 1946. Through a mistake by Herman Goldstine, who distributed a memo which was named only with the name of the ENIAC-project member John von Neumann and who omitted the names of Eckert and Mauchly, the architecture is unjustified known as the *von Neumann Computer*. At the same time as the work on ENIAC, Mark Aiken from Harvard University was building an electromechanical computer called the Mark-I, whose processor-memory architecture is today known as the *Harvard architecture*. Both terms are used today to distinguish between machines with a single main memory used for instructions and data together (von Neumann) and separate memories for instruction and for data (Harvard).

Apart from memory, a basic structure principle has become a standard for machines – the organization in a data processing and a controlling part. Because of the view of data throughput or data flow and the according control signals or the control flow, these parts are called *data path (DP)* and *control path (CP)*. They are the fundamental components of a processor or a central processing unit (CPU). As a representative example for various kinds of DPs, the basic structure and purposes of an 8bit example (Fig. 12) is explained. This DP is proposed in [41].

A DP is a combination of combinational and sequential elements. The ALU serves the arithmetical or logical operations with two operands A and B. An Operation can e.g. be a data transfer which is needed for MOV instructions, which may also require the addition for offset-operations, increment- or decrement-operations for loop-calculations. Possible are also logic operations like AND, OR, XOR, etc. to realize the according instruction directly or to perform mask-operations. The operation is controlled by signals ALU_F[2:0] and Cin. The sources of A and B are selected by multiplexers through signals A[2:0] and B[2:0]. Sources are e.g. data registers from the register-file or a data vector (IN_DATA[7:0]) from an input port. The result vector from the ALU can be shifted or rotated - controlled by H[2:0]. According to ALU operation, some flags (V = overflow, Z = zero, S = sign, C = Carry) can be set. These flags are fed back to the CP. The result vector of the ALU/shifter circuits can be read at the output port S[7:0] or it can be stored in a register. The destination register is selected at the time of writing with control signals D[2:0]. Control signals are summarized in the control word (CW). The data flow is controlled through different CWs for every time generated by the CP. A data flow graph is used as an abstraction for data operations and the throughput within the DP.

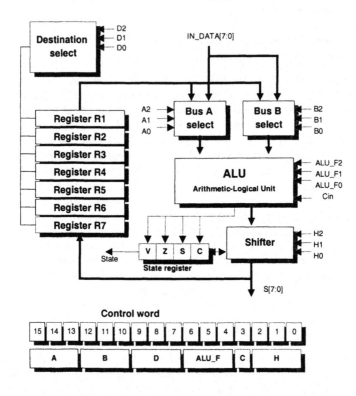

Fig. 12. Basic Structure of a Data Path

The main function, of the CP is to organize the execution of a program as a sequence of (macro-) instructions. Every instruction is subdivide into micro-instructions or -operations. Micro-operations are each associated with specific signals to control elementary functionalities such as register loading, memory reading/writing, ALU-function and so one. Basic components of a CP (see also Fig. 13) are a program-counter (PC), and a memory address register (MAR), which contains the actual address pointer (pt). Furthermore, a memory buffer register (MBR) may be necessary for memory access (read, write) operations.

The central building block is the control logic (CL). It may be implemented hardwired or micro-programmed. A instruction register (IR) with an instruction decoder (ID) delivers the instruction variable q_k. A sequencer or a timer generate time-signals t_i. The CL generates control signals y_x, often structured as a control word, depending on input bits from decoded instructions, timer signals and fed-back flag signals c_i from the data path. A general purpose CP contains also a stack-pointer (SP) to address a reserved memory area called the stack. Furthermore, an interrupt controller is usually installed to control exceptions, break request from the operating system or external hardware. It is also necessary for handling conflicts, e.g. associated with failures in memory access (e.g. in case of page faults) by inserting wait cycles.

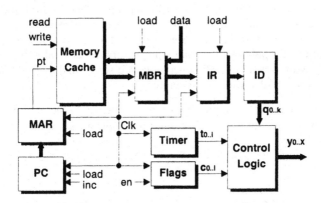

Fig. 13. Basic structure of a Control Path

The control flow for one instruction is divided into the fetch and the execution phase. Micro-instructions are assigned to the according phase. Always the same micro-instructions are used for the instruction fetch. In the execution phase, control signals differ between instructions. More detailed information about control flow and how it is associated with the processor state machine is given in chapter 4.

The relevant control flow principle is strongly dependent on the processor type. In recent architectures, the control flow is highly optimized. Examples for control-flow relevant performance enhancing operations are instructions pre-fetch, pipelined program execution, shortened micro-instruction sequences with additional hardware (RISC-processors), branch prediction and many more.

2.2.2 Processor Types

The following explanations would give a short introduction into different types of processors. Since the early computer developed by Konrad Zuse, various processor architectures for different applications have been developed. In 1966, Flynn proposed a simple model for a coarse grained classification of processors or computers [42].

1. *Single instruction Stream, Single Data Stream (SISD)*
2. *Single instruction Stream, Multiple Data Stream (SIMD)*
3. *Multiple instruction Stream, Single Data Stream (MISD)*
4. *Multiple instruction Stream, Multiple Data Stream (MIMD)*

A SISD-processor is a universal machine with one instruction flow and an accordingly sequential data flow. Most of early microprocessors (e.g. Intel's 80x86 up to the

80486), also pipelined RISC and CISC processors (e.g. DLX and DEC/VAX), CPU-cores of micro-controllers (e.g. Motorola's HC05/11/08/12) are members of this family. In a SIMD architecture, one instruction flow controls multiple concurrent data flow. Vector-processors and array machines can be assigned to this class. A constellation of a processor plus a co-processor, e.g. for floating point operation, can be seen as a SIMD machine. In a MISD, one data flow is controlled by multiple controllers. This principle can be found in UNIX-pipe operations. The MIMD-principle with concurrent control sequences and data processing found a widespread use in processors for high performance application. Today's processors in personal computers plus the according processors for multimedia operations are some kind of MIMD-processors. This class now consist of various architectures.

Fig. 14 tries to arrange different processor types according to the 'von Neumann'- and the 'Harvard'-principle, but it does not claim for completeness. Some types overlap in some characteristics.

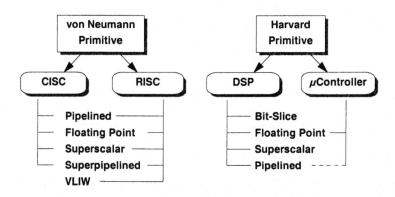

Fig. 14. Processor type classification

For a long time, computer architecture worried about the "semantic gap" between high-level languages such as PASCAL and machine instructions. It was common sense that a small semantic gap would result in good computer performance. Hence several architectures such as IBM's 360 and 370 and, most notably, the DEC/VAX architecture supported a long list of complex machine instructions. Microprocessor architectures of the 1970s and early 1980s also followed the principles. Many types of today's microprocessors are still CISC-processors.

The main reason for complex – and often by compilers not completely used – instruction sets in CISCs (mostly > 250 instructions) is the compatibility with earlier program or processor versions [39]. CISC-processors are very flexible and efficient: A basic instruction set exists in upward-compatible processor-families plus instructions with additional functionality. New sequences of micro-instructions are combined into more powerful and faster macro-instructions. But large and error-susceptible micro-programs, complex address calculation and a needful memory access protection make processors with smaller instruction sets necessary for some applications. Classical examples for CISC-machines are the IBM370/168 or VAX-11/780. Newer CISC-types are e.g. processors from Intel- or AMD for personal computers. But recent Intel-architecture are not really new CISC-machines. A performance improvement was reached with a decomposition of x86-instructions into fragments which are executed in parallel. Special features implemented to enhance performance are pipelining or super-pipelining, super-scalar architecture or floating-point units. Most of these principles were first implemented in high-end CISC machines of the 1970s. In VLIW architectures, data operations are sorted in advance by the compiler in order to execute them in parallel units. With the design of RISC-processors, architects tried to realize an instruction in one cycle (CPI = Clocks Per Instruction = 1): In this architecture, only basically needed machine instructions are implemented, whose flow of micro-operations is highly optimized. According to their evolution, RISC-Architectures can be divide into three generations [43]:

1. *RISC – Generation: - first developments by Universities Stanford (MIPS) and Berkeley (RISC I and RISC II) and IBM (801) with low complexity, 30-50 instructions*
2. *RISC – Generation: - more powerful sets with ca. 100 instructions, floating point operations, embedded memory management units, examples are Am29000, SUN SPARC, MIPS, etc.*
3. *RISC – Generation: - super-scalar (IBM/6000, i860) and super-pipelined (CPI < 1)*

A classification from a practical point of view is difficult because of various features of the target systems: costs, speed or clock frequency, development software and compiler, dependability and so on. For current and future embedded systems, also architectures with high-end performance will be used. A today's point at issue is a standardization for embedded processors or for such processor cores [44], [45], [46] and the respective dependability.

2.2.3 Fault Effects in Processors

The investigation of the error behavior of an embedded system – respective an embedded processor was the objective of many recent research efforts. Fault injection techniques have become a popular approach to evaluate and improve the dependability of embedded processor-based systems [24], [35], [47], [48]. Permanent and transient faults may cause different effects in embedded processors. Fault injection experiments [35] determined latent errors as the largest part of all fault groups. Effective errors often results in processor exception states [47].

To give an introduction into the principles and functions of proposed on-line check structures, this section presents examples for effective and latent errors which have an impact on control and / or data flow. An universal description of fault effects is hardly possible because of different processor architectures, applications and various system-specific constraints.

The Fig. 15 serves to explain different possible faults (*Fx*) in a processor control path structure.

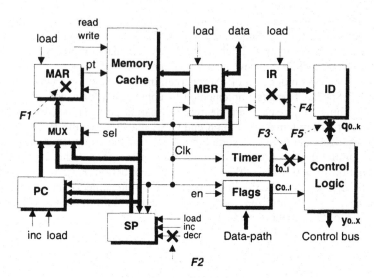

Fig. 15. Examples For Faults in CP-Structures

Fault F1:   A register fault within the memory address register (MAR) is assumed. The address pointer selects a wrong address in the memory or cache unit. If the faulty pointer addresses a protected area or overflows memory area, an exception may be occurred. Therefore this fault causes an *effective error*. An *overwritten error* exists if the memory is not read or written, and the MAR is loaded within the next cycle (condition: transient fault). If an instruction has to be read and the pointer addresses an operand instead an op-code (operation code), a *latent error* occurred. The latency depends on the duration for implemented illegal op-code detection.

Fault F2:   An error on the decrement control line (decr) of the control register SP (stack pointer) is assumed. The decr-signal is used to address the next stack address within the μOp (micro-operation) sequences (y$_x$) for PUSH or BRANCH instructions. An *effective error* is given, for instance, if the stack pointer addresses a wrong data word instead an op-code. If a component for illegal op-code-detection is implemented, an exception handling routine is started. An *overwritten error* can be assumed in the case of a ft1 fault at the line if decr is anyway active. If this signal is flipping to zero, the earlier address will be overwritten. If decr is stuck at zero, entire data will be stored at the same stack address. In this case a *latent error* exists if stack data will be read back

Fault F3:   A time-signal line error is assumed. A hard-wired control logic generates control signals dependent on instruction-, time- and flag-signals. An *effective error* exists if a timer reset is executed at the wrong time. This effect can occurre e.g. if the last time variable of a μOp sequence is flipped to one. Because of incomplete sequence an exception may take place. If more than one time condition is active for the same instruction, additional μOps will be executed. Possibilities for *overwritten* and *latent errors* are obvious.

Fault F4:   Effects of faults in the IR (instruction register) are similar to F3. The instruction is one of the variables for the execution of μOp sequences. With an illegal op-code detection unit *effective errors* can be detected immediately. But instruction sets with a small Hamming-distance between op-codes are dangerous because of possible undetected errors. For instance, the op-code JNZ (jump not zero) = 11000010 of the Intel 8085-CPU shifts to RNZ (return not zero) = 11000000 if bit-1 was upset. The instruction TXS (transfer from index register X to stack-pointer) = 00110101 of Motorola's HC11 is replaced with BCLR (clear bit(s) in memory) = 00010101 if bit-6 flips to zero.

Fault F5:   Faults at this line can result in the start of more than one μOp sequences if one or more inactive lines flip to one. If the active q-line flips to zero within a cycle, corresponding μOps are not executed.

Methods to detect effective and latent errors in registers are proposed in section 3.2 and 3.3 A special problem in on-line testing/checking is obvious from these examples: An observation of registers or data manipulating logic, for instance with special codes or with duplication is useless in the case of control errors. Therefore, the test, the check, or the observation of the processor-operation has to be considered as the observation of the co-operation of two finite state machines (FSM): the *data flow graph* controlled by the *control flow graph*. All processor test strategies have to take this assumption into account. The starting point for proposed techniques of this thesis is the distinction of possible processor faults into *component* and *control* faults.

Component faults: - Decoder faults (e.g. register select)
                     - MUX faults (e.g. bus select)
                     - Data storage (e.g. register cell stuck-at, bridge or bit-flip)
                     - Data transfer (e.g. data line stuck-at, bridge or bit-flip)

Control faults: - Register address code (e.g. no or another register is selected)
                     - MUX select faults (e.g. wrong bus is selected)
                     - Register load / enable (e.g. no rising edge if clock is gated)
                     - Data manipulation (e.g. ALU-control faults)
                     - μOp faults (e.g. inactive or additional active μOps)

Most of component faults may be mainly assigned to data flow graph except for control-relevant components (e.g., instruction register, control logic). Control faults impact both graphs with effects which are described in the examples above.

3. On-line Check Technology for Processor Components

Production test cannot ensure the level of dependability needed in safety-critical systems or systems in hostile environment. The reason is that transient effects or changed system parameters are not detectable in advance by production test techniques.

The time diagram outlined in Fig. 16 explains the stages from an effective fault to a system failure. This diagram is based on a figure from Clark and Pradhan in [50]. It shows that an early fault detection may avoid a system failure if the time for a fault-tolerance mechanism is sufficient. Therefore, on-line error detection in digital circuits is a must to fulfill the demands for the dependability in current and future embedded systems.

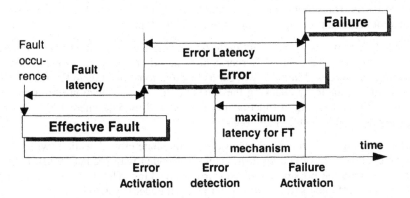

Fig. 16. Time Behavior of a Fault, an Error and a Failure

Sections 3.1 and 4.1 give a brief overview of on-line test or check techniques in digital circuits. Sections 3.2 to 3.3 and 4.2 to 4.3 present extended and new on-line techniques for the observation of components and the according control signal flow for data operations in embedded processors.

3.1 State of the Art

On-line checking techniques have been proposed and have been used for digital circuits for several years. The simplest way for an on-line, respectively concurrent testing or checking is to duplicate the relevant devices and compare signals or data. Various approaches from FT-techniques are used to detect errors. Duplication and comparison or triplication and voting provide a solution for all digital designs, especially processor- or controller-based designs at the expense of a high overhead. The advantage is the ability to detect arbitrary errors (exclusive design or specification errors). The disadvantage is the overhead which is more than 100 % of the original circuit. A further disadvantage is the ratio of yield versus the required chip area. A duplicated or triplicated circuit results in reduced production yield, which is roughly inverse proportional to the chip area [50]. But with just total standard processor cores available as black boxes (IP-cores), a duplication or triplication of the processor structure is inevitable for an error detection or fault tolerance. A further class of error detection circuits is the *two-rail logic*, where the original and the duplicated circuit are implemented with inverse outputs [51].

A gain in efficiency is achieved with the modification of circuit duplicates. The *pseudo-duplication* – proposed in [52] – is a method to process data twice in succession by the same circuit, but along different data paths. Here, the longer processing time is the overhead. Therefore, this pseudo-duplication is only suitable for on-line checking if it is used with duplication in a mixed manner [53].

More cost-effective solutions are the objective of further investigations in error-detecting codes. A known example is the parity code which adds one check bit for even or odd parity. Hamming-codes are often used for fault detection and also correction in communication protocols, for instance the TCP/IP protocol.

Berger code [54] provides a good solution to detect single and unidirectional multiple bit faults in combinatorial circuits. Berger code is based on counting zeros or ones in the according data vector. Faults may occur as bi-directional bit flips in the vector. So this fault is undetectable by checking the Berger code. A modification into a *monotone* circuit with the keeping of functionality is proposed in [55], where 100% of single faults are detectable with Berger codes.

The goal of investigations for this thesis was an immediate error detection (within the same clock cycle). A lot of coding techniques is provided with prediction algorithms in order to enhance the possibility for concurrent checking. The difficulty is to find the best and most efficient solution for the target (embedded) system [56].

The practical use of codes for on-line or concurrent error detection can be classified into data and hardware redundancy. With data redundancy, check-bits are added to the data vector. An other technique provides source or channel coding (e.g. with cyclic coding). Hardware redundancy is often used for data coding, for code prediction or for the comparison of both. Examples are parity or group-parity prediction [57], [58]. Berger code prediction is a further technique with an overhead less than duplication to detect errors through the comparison of pre-calculated bits and the real code. An approach to Berger code prediction for an arithmetical-logical-unit (ALU) is proposed in [59]. A strongly fault secure ALU was designed, which is based on Berger (code) check prediction (BCP). Section 3.2 gives detailed information about this principle and about proprietary modifications for on-line check of data containing (e.g. registers, stack) and data manipulating components (e.g. shifters, floating-point units).

3.2 Component On-line Check Using Extended Berger Code Prediction

3.2.1 BCP for Integer Data-Paths

The BCP ALU proposed in [59] was designed to observe integer arithmetic and logical functions of data paths. In this paper, the mathematical foundation concerning the prediction of Berger code was developed.

For a given operation $F = A$ op B, the operands A and B are Berger encoded with checks A_c and B_c, and the result is Berger encoded with F_c. Table 2 shows the basic equations to predict the Berger-code according to integer ALU-function – controlled by $S_{2..0}$ and c_{in} [41].

Table 2. ALU functions and according Berger Code Check Formulas [59]

S_2	S_1	S_0	c_{in}	Function	Berger Check Symbol F_c
0	0	0	0	$F = A$	$F_c = A_c - C_c - c_{in} + c_{out} + n$
0	0	0	1	$F = A + 1$	$F_c = A_c - C_c - c_{in} + c_{out} + n$
0	0	1	0	$F = A + B$	$F_c = A_c + B_c - C_c - c_{in} + c_{out}$
0	0	1	1	$F = A + B + 1$	$F_c = A_c + B_c - C_c - c_{in} + c_{out}$
0	1	0	0	$F = A - B - 1$	$F_c = A_c - B_c - C_c - /c_{in} + c_{out} + n$
0	1	0	1	$F = A - B$	$F_c = A_c - B_c - C_c - /c_{in} + c_{out} + n$
0	1	1	0	$F = A - 1$	$F_c = A_c - C_c - /c_{in} + c_{out}$
0	1	1	1	$F = A$	$F_c = A_c - C_c - /c_{in} + c_{out}$
1	0	0	X	$F = A$ or B	$F_c = A_c + B_c - (A$ and $B)_c$
1	0	1	X	$F = A$ xor B	$F_c = A_c + B_c - 2(A$ or $B)_c + n$
1	1	0	X	$F = A$ and B	$F_c = A_c + B_c - (A$ or $B)_c$
1	1	1	X	$F = $ not A	$F_c = n - A_c$

$S_{2..0} \wedge c_{in}$ ... ALU control signals according to [41]

F .... ALU-result;

A .... Operand A;

B .... Operand B;

C .... ALU-internal carry-vector;

X_c .... Berger-code of X (number of '0's);

c_{in} .... Carry in bit; $/c_{in}$ ... inverted carry in bit;

c_{out} .... Carry out bit;

n .... Bit width of operands $(n - X_c = N(X)$: number of '1's) ;

An extension was to include shift and rotate operation (e.g. through combinatorial shifter or accumulator register). The Berger code of these functions can be built for '0'-counting with the following formulas:

Shift right:	$F_C = A_C + A_L$
Shift left:	$F_C = A_C + A_M$
Rotate left/right:	$F_C = A_C$

The indices L and M represent the least and the most significant bit of data word.

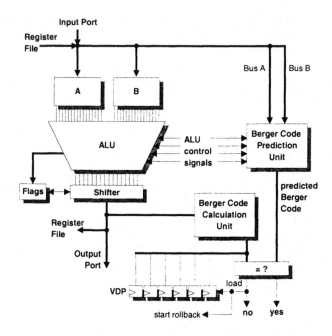

Fig. 17. Basic Structure of BCP for a simple Datapath

If the BCP checker (consisting of the BC calculation unit and comparator) detects a difference between predicted and calculated Berger code, the word will be stored in the *error vector of the data path* (VDP) as a representing error vector in the case of an error-caused DP fault. This vector is further used for a distinction of the occurred fault into the transient or the permanent class. The basic idea of this classification is outlined in chapter 5.

The principle of BCP was extended to observe also other data path components such as register file, shifter, etc. (see also Fig. 18). We include the register check by Berger encoding of every register content in the time of register writing. This Berger code (calculated with BC unit 2) is stored in an additional buffer which is dependent on register widths (e.g. 4 bit for a 16 bit register). If a register is read for a data operation, the register content is coded with BCP unit (BC unit 1). Both vectors are compared. A fault has occurred in the register or in the BC register if a difference is detected. The re-calculated Berger code of the current register content is stored in the fault-representing vector VDP for further error classification.

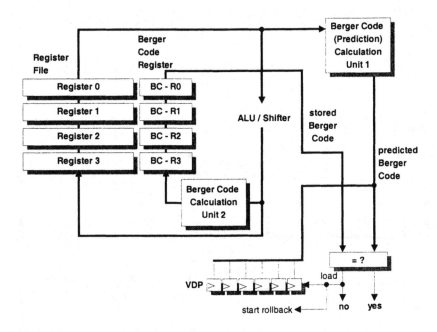

Fig. 18. BC-Observation of a Register File

3.2.2 BCP for Floating-Point Components

Current general purpose processors support floating point data operations with various precision formats (IEEE standard 754). At present, published methods for the on-line observation of DP-components are limited to integer operations [59]. In a recent investigation we modified the BCP in order to observe single (32 bit) and double precision (64 bit) floating point units (FPU) [21]. Formulas in Table 2 have to be adapted for extra operations for sign, biased exponent and fraction calculations. The following example for a pipelined addition-subtraction FPU (the structure is shown in Fig. 20) outlines the basic principle for an on-line observation.

We consider the (usual) positive normalized floating point representation according to standard IEEE 754. A number $\pm 1 \cdot 2^{EXP-127}$ for single precision is interpreted as a 32-bit word - outlined in Fig. 19 (n=32):

Fig. 19. Single Precision Floating Point Representation

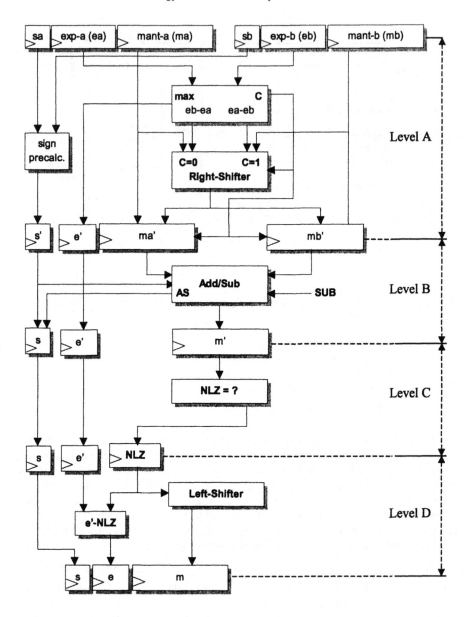

Fig. 20. Basic Structure of a Pipelined Add-Sub FPU

A floating point unit compares first exponents of both operands. The highest exponent is the temporary result exponent (Level A). The addition (SUB=0) or, respectively, the subtraction (SUB=1) of a FPU starts with the exponent (ea or eb) adoption and the according right-shift of fraction bits of the smaller operand ($\max\{$ea-eb, eb-ea$\}$) (Level A). Bit C indicates the result of the comparison and controls the swap unit (ea≥eb → C=0: mb *is shifted right;* ea<eb → C=1: ma *is shifted right*). Bits NBa and NBb represent the one before the decimal point, which is omitted in the binary representation. They have to be considered for real data operation in the *Add/Sub-unit* (Level B). NBa and NBb indicate if an operand (ma or mb) is shifted due to the adoption. The number of right-shifts is represented with rsh. AS is the negated carry-out of the add/sub-unit. It is followed by a re-normalization. Here the number of leading zeros (NLZ) is counted (Level C) and the fraction is left-shifted accordingly.

Based from formulas for addition/subtraction in Tab. 2, the prediction of BC for the result fraction has to consider different operations steps and adoptions and can be carried out with following formulas according control bit SUB:

Addition ($SUB = 0$):

$$m_C = \left[ma_C + \left(\sum_{n=0}^{rsh-1} (C \wedge ma_n) \right) - C + \overline{NBa} \right] + \left[mb_C + \left(\sum_{n=0}^{rsh-1} \left(\overline{C} \wedge mb_n \right) \right) - \overline{C} + \overline{NBb} \right] - C_C + \overline{AS}$$

Subtr. ($SUB =1$):

$$m_C = \left[ma_C + \left(\sum_{n=0}^{rsh-1} (C \wedge ma_n) \right) - C + \overline{NBa} \right] - \left[mb_C + \left(\sum_{n=0}^{rsh-1} \left(\overline{C} \wedge mb_n \right) \right) - \overline{C} + \overline{NBb} \right] - C_C + n - \overline{c_{in}} + \overline{AS}$$

m_C	... Berger code (BC) of result mantissa
ma_C/mb_C	... BC of operand A / B mantissa
C	... Identificator for exponent comparison
rsh	... number of mantissa right-shifts
C_C	... Internal carries from Add-Sub-unit
NBa/NBb	... Normalize-bit or 'virtual bit' ($0.11.. \rightarrow NB = 0$; $1.11.. \rightarrow NB = 1$)
$\overline{c_{in}}$	... not carry in bit
AS	... $\overline{c_{out}}$ from Add-Sub-unit
n	... bit widht

The term $\left(\sum_{n=0}^{rsh-1} (C \wedge ma_n) \right)$ and, respectively, $\left(\sum_{n=0}^{rsh-1} \left(\overline{C} \wedge mb_n \right) \right)$ consider 'right-out-shifted' bits in case of an operand adoption. If the smaller operand is right-shifted, a number of bits (rsh) may be shifted out and the BC has to be decrease accordingly the number of 'lost' zero's. At the same time, the same number of 'out-shifted' bits is refilled with zeros at the most significant bit positions. According the positive normalized representation, the mantissa is represented without the '*1.*'. If an (smaller) operand is adopted (right-shifted), it has to be considered (one zero less in the BC). Bit C identifies adopted mantissa.

So, the 'left-in-shifted' one is considered with $... - C$ respective $... - \overline{C}$. On the other hand, full representations of ma and mb in the add/sub-unit include full vectors. Bits NBa and NBb serves expansion of operands (*0.* or *1.*). The BC for the mantissa must be adopted accordingly. The BC of the internal carry-vector (C_C) is obtained from the add/sub-unit in level B. The signal AS represents the negated carry-out of the add/sub-unit.

The following example illustrate the change of BC in the case of an operand adoption: Let assume two single-precision numbers (32 bit), which have to be added (SUB = 0):

$A = 43.1252441406_{dec}$ $= 101011.001000000001_{bin}$
$= 1.01011001000000001 * 2^5{}_{bin}$

$B = 0.133301735_{dec}$ $= 0.00100010001000000001_{bin}$
$= 1.00010001000000001 * 2^{-3}{}_{bin}$

The representation in IEEE 754 floating-point format is as follow:

A: $\boxed{0|10000100|0101100100000000010..000}$
B: $\boxed{0|01111100|0001000100000000010..000}$

The exponent subtraction result is $rsh = 8$. B has the smaller exponent ($C = 0$, $NBa = 1$, $NBb = 0$). It must be shifted right for 8 bits. (Remark: The considera-tion of the mantissa Berger code is extended to 24 bits $\rightarrow$ BC' (plus the 'virtual bit'), because real adder process also this bit-width.)

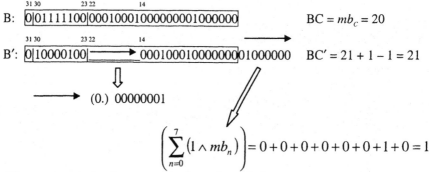

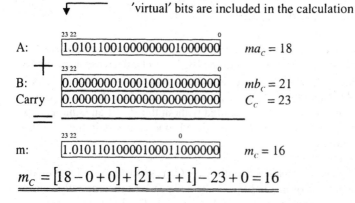

After exponent adoption, ma and mb can be added:

$m_C = [18-0+0]+[21-1+1]-23+0 = 16$

If a result mantissa has the form 0.000101 or similar, it must be re-normalized to 1.01. Therefore, the number of leading zeros (NLZ) is counted. NLZ is equal to necessary 'left-out shifted' zero's. For the calculation of the result-mantissa-BC m_C, it has no effect because at least-significant bit position exact NLZ zeros are 'shifted in'.

With a result mantissa form 11.010... an add/sub-unit overflow has occurred (add_of = 1). For this case, an 1-bit right-shift is provided. If the least-significant (out-shifted) output bit from add/sub-unit is zero (AS_out(0)), it has to be considered in prediction formulas for the result mantissa. If the 'virtual bit' of the positive-normalized floating point representation is shifted right into the mantissa, it has to be considered actually in the final BC-calculation.

Because $0 = -C + \overline{NBa} = -\overline{C} + \overline{NBb}$ and previously explained adoptions, the formula for a floating point addition can be extended as follows:

Addition ($SUB = 0$):

$$m_C = \left[ma_C + \left(\sum_{n=0}^{rsh-1}(C \wedge ma_n) \right) \right] + \left[mb_C + \left(\sum_{n=0}^{rsh-1}(\overline{C} \wedge mb_n) \right) \right] - C_C + \overline{AS} - \left[add\_of \wedge \overline{AS\_out(0)} \right]$$

For a subtraction, two cases have to be considered:

1. Subtraction (SUB =1): *if the result is positive* (carry[23] =1 $\rightarrow$ $\overline{AS}$ = 0)

It is possible to replace the term $\left[-C_C + n \right]$ with $\left[+N(C) \right]$ (one-count of internal carry-vector).

$$m_C = \left[ma_C + \left(\sum_{n=0}^{rsh-1}(C \wedge ma_n) \right) \right] - \left[mb_C + \left(\sum_{n=0}^{rsh-1}(\overline{C} \wedge mb_n) \right) \right] + N(C) - \overline{c_{in}} + \overline{AS}...$$

$$...- \left[add\_of \wedge \overline{AS\_out(0)} \right]$$

2. Subtraction (SUB =1): *if the result is negative* (carry[23] =0 $\rightarrow$ $\overline{AS}$ =1)

If the result is negative, an additional two's complement has to be built to obtain the real mantissa. But the previous formula has to be extended for this case. Because the two's complement is a one's complement plus 1, the formula is extended as an BC-calculation of an addition. Let be the (single precision) result of first subtraction case = m_C', then we get for the one's complement [24 − m_C]. An addition with binary one (000...001) means for BC-calculation an addition of 23. The internal carries ($C2_C$) and the carry-out signal ($c2_{out}$) of the two's complement unit has also to be considered:

$$m_C = (24 - m_C') + 23 - C2_C + c2_{out}$$

The summarized prediction formula for the mantissa Berger code is configured for single-precision subtraction (second case) as follow:

$$m_C = 47 - \left[ma_C + \left(\sum_{n=0}^{rsh-1}(C \wedge ma_n)\right)\right] - \left[mb_C + \left(\sum_{n=0}^{rsh-1}(\overline{C} \wedge mb_n)\right)\right] + N(C) - \overline{c_{in}} + \overline{AS}...$$

$$..... - \left[add\_of \wedge \overline{AS\_out(0)}\right] - C2_C + c2_{out}$$

With the following example, this formula will be tried: Let us assume two single-precision numbers (32 bit), which have to be subtracted (SUB = 1):

$A = -1.2509765625_{dec} = -1.0100000001_{bin} = -1.0100000001 * 2^0{}_{bin}$

$B = +5678.0625_{dec} = +1011000101110.0001_{bin} = +1.0110001011100001 * 2^{12}{}_{bin}$

The representation in IEEE 754 floating-point format is as follow:

A: $\boxed{1|01111111|0100000001000..000}$ B: $\boxed{0|10001011|01100010111000100..000}$

The exponent subtraction result is rsh = 12. A has the smaller exponent (C = 1, NBa = 0, NBb = 1). It must be shifted right by 12 bits.

31 30   23 22   10   0
A : $\boxed{1|01111111|0100000001000000000000000}$ $BC = ma_C = 21$

31 30   23 22   10   0   ⟶
A': $\boxed{0|10000100|\qquad\qquad\qquad 0100000001\,0000000000000}$ $BC' = 21 + 1 - 1 = 21$

⇓   ⇓

⟶ (0.) 000000000001 $\left(\sum_{n=0}^{11}(1 \wedge ma_n)\right) = 12 \cdot 0 = 0$

After exponent adoption, *ma* and *mb* can be subtracted:

⌐——————— 'virtual' bits are included in the calculation
↓

23 22   0
A: $\boxed{0.000000000000101000000010}$ $ma_C = 21$

23 22   0
B: $\boxed{1.0110001011100001000000}$ $mb_C = 16$
Carry $\boxed{0.000000000000111001111111}$ $C_C = 14; N(C) = 10$

23 22   0
m': $\boxed{0.100111010011001100000010}$ $m_C'= 21 - 16 + 10 - 0 + 0 = 14$
↑——————— carry[23]=0 → two's complement

23 22   0
C2: $\boxed{0.000000000000000000000001}$ $C2_C = 23; c2_{out} = 0$

23 22   0
m: $\boxed{1.011000101100110011111110}$ $m_C = 47 - 14 - 23 + 0 = 10$

The prediction of the BC for the result-sign is trivial and can calculated as follow:

$$\overline{s_C} = \left(sa \wedge \overline{AS}\right) \vee \left(sb \wedge \overline{SUB} \wedge AS\right) \vee \left(\overline{sb} \wedge SUB \wedge AS\right)$$

The BC of the result-exponent e can derived first from the BC of the greatest exponent of ma or mb. Finally, an adoption has to be carried out according to the NLZ after re-normalization:

$$e_C = \left[\max\{(ea),(eb)\} - add\_of\right]_C - NLZ_C - C(NLZ)_C + n - \overline{c_{in}} + c_{out}$$

The term $N(C) = n - C(NLZ)_C$ represents the number of '1's in the internal carry-vector. So the prediction formula can be written in the following form:

$$e_C = \left[\max\{(ea),(eb)\} - add\_of\right]_C - NLZ_C - N(C) - \overline{c_{in}} + c_{out}$$

A c_{out} in the exponent calculation corresponds to an exponent-underflow and would usually set off an exception.

The formulas above represent the prediction logic for the whole FPU. For a finer-granular on-line observation of every stage, these rules can be partitioned according to the actually partial function of the stage. Registers can be included in the check technique as described for integer DPs. The overhead is obviously higher, but an error-localization is more precise.

According the regulations of IEEE standard 754 or possible design- or custom-specific constraints of a FPU-architecture, prediction formulas can be easy adopted. For instance, if one or more rounding steps are included into floating point operations, the formulas above are easily extendable by according handling of 'right-out-shifted' bits.

3.2.3 Results

The shareable use of BCP-observation for ALU/shifter and register files provides a good solution to small integer data-paths (8/16-bit and register file with max. 16 register). Beyond this level, data path overhead can reach an unacceptable level. The hardware overhead for the on-line observation of different integer ALU-designs was investigated with various experiments and implementations with the same functionality but different bit-ranges (see also Tab. 3 and 4).

Implementations vary according to their design-flow because of differently obtained gate counts. Viewlogic's WVO 7.5™ (now Innoveda's ePD 1.1™) was used as a design environment. It allows gate-level, RTL-design or the synthesis of VHDL/Verilog-descriptions (Synopsys' FPGA Express™). Experiences have shown that synthesized circuits have often a higher gate count than 'hand-made' schematics. Various synthesis options can impact the final circuit: timing constraints, optimization for time or area, different algorithms for the removing of redundancies, etc.

To investigate different implementation variants, we consider synthesized VHDL (optimized for chip area), a gate-level description of an ALU with a carry-ripple-adder and with a carry-look-ahead-adder (CLA). The first row of Tab. 3 shows the gate count of a synthesized VHDL-description of an ALU. Rows two and tree contain data for the gate level design. All circuits are mapped to a standard logic library from Lattice Semiconductor Corporation [60] in order to obtain a good estimation for the necessary gate count.

Table 3. Gate Count for various ALU-Designs, Shifters and BCP-units

Integer worth length	8-bit	16-bit	32-bit	64-bit
Synthesized ALU (based on structural VHDL)	196 gates	396 gates	796 gates	1596 gates
ALU logic design (without CLA)	110 gates	230 gates	454 gates	865 gates
ALU design with carry Look ahead adder (CLA)	138 gates (8-bit CLA)	335 gates (16-bit CLA)	675 gates (16-bit CLA)	1345 gates (16-bit CLA)
Combinatorial shifter	84 gates	118 gates	230 gates	452 gates
BC prediction unit	222 gates	424 gates	824 gates	1620 gates
BC unit + Comparator	35 gates	83 gates	183 gates	387 gates
Complete BCP unit	257 gates	507 gates	1007 gates	2007 gates

Experiments have shown that the hardware overhead for complete BCP-units (ALU-checker plus additional registers) can reach 100% and more for 32 bit and wider integer components. The RB multiplexers outlined in Tab. 4 are included into the overhead calculation because they are needed to carry out the micro-rollback (see also chapter 5).

Table 4. Gate Count for Complete BCP-units (Fig. 17 and 18)

Integer worth length	8-bit	16-bit	32-bit
DP (ALU, shifter and 7 registers) without BCP	554 gates	904 gates	1682 gates
DP with BCP observation (plus 'RB Multiplexors')	1002 gates (1338 gates)	1411 gates (1891 gates)	2824 gates (3784 gates)
Overhead (plus 'RB Multiplexors')	81 % (141 %)	56 % (109 %)	68 % (125 %)

The reason for the overhead in table 4 is the amount of needed '0'-counters. Various synthesized VHDL-descriptions and optimized logic implementations for these counters have reached nearly identical results. To reduce the overhead for the complete BCP-concept in integer DPs, the use of *Cross-parity-prediction (CPP)* is proposed as an alternative for register file on-line check (see also section 3.3).

The modified Berger-Code prediction and check unit for addition/subtraction floating-point-units for single precision (32-bit) needs an overhead of 2834 and for double precision (64-bit) 4770 gates. The relative overhead amounts here are to approximately 38% for the 32-bit- and 18% for the 64-bit-FPU (depending on the FPU-implementation).

3.3 Component On-line Check with Cross-Parity Check

3.3.1 Introduction

The possibilities of parity check in processor registers or register files were investigated in order to obtain a smaller gate count for the whole on-line check scheme. The decision for the commonly used check strategies is a compromise between adequate error coverage and acceptable overhead [56].

Derived from error detecting codes in communication techniques, the principle of *Cross-parity prediction* (CPP) [21], [78] is introduced for register on-line check or concurrent error detection.

Parity-checking strategies are well known for an efficient single fault detection in registers or data words. Parity coding is based on calculation of even or odd parity for data of word length N. If the number of binary '1'-valued bits X within the data word (N-1 ≥ X ≥ 0) is divisible by two, the parity is even otherwise odd. The parity can be calculated with XOR- (Exclusive OR = $\oplus$), respectively with an XNOR-junction (Exclusive Not-OR = $\odot$).

Table 5. Truth table for even and odd parity

A	B	C	Even Parity (XNOR)	Odd Parity (XOR)
0	0	0	1	0
0	0	1	0	1
0	1	0	0	1
0	1	1	1	0
1	0	0	0	1
1	0	1	1	0
1	1	0	1	0
1	1	1	0	1

A couple of publications has proposed the principle of parity prediction or group-parity prediction. These techniques deal with the pre-calculation of the result parity according to an arithmetic operation (e.g. binary addition). A check of predicted and real parity can easily detect single-bit faults (B=1; 2*B−1) and multiple-bit faults (B>1) with the type (2*B+1). The disadvantage is here the missing recognizability of by-2-divisible multiple-bit faults (even multiplicity). The example for an 8x8-bit register file in Fig. 21 illustrate this fact. Faults in register 7 and 5 can be detected by parity-check. But faults in register 6 and 3 remain undetected.

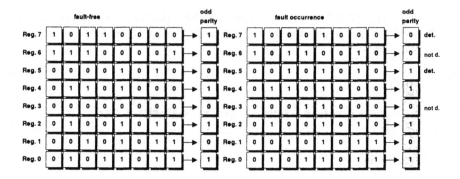

Fig. 21. Limitation of Simple Parity check

To detect multiple faults as in registers 6 and 3, the simple parity calculation was extended to the calculation of row- and column-parities. The parity-coding of rows and columns in data packets and the check after the transfer allows an error detection and a localization within a 'hair cross' (see Fig. 22). The double-fault in register 3 (Fig. 21) is easily detectable.

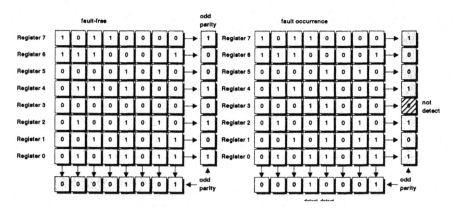

Fig. 22. Row- and Column-Parity check

But if a multiple fault has occurred in register 4 and 3 as in the illustration in Fig. 23, it can not be detected with this strategy. This is also valid for 'symmetric' multiple faults of the type (2*B)*(2*register).

To detect multiple faults with this structure, the calculation of the *diagonal-parity* is introduced. According to the 'little endian' mode, the diagonal parity can be calculated from the most significant bit of the most significant register to the least significant bit of the least significant register (top-left to down-right or even the other way round).

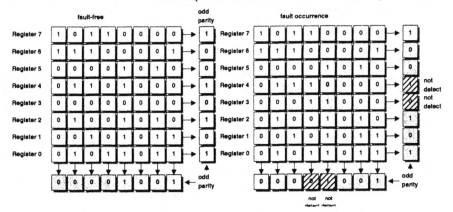

Fig. 23. Limitation of Row- and Column-Parity check

The combined check of row-, column- and diagonal-parity is the so called *cross-parity check* [21]. If Y is the bit-width of a register and X is the number of registers, the Cross-Parity is composed from the row-parity vector r [(X-1) : 0], the column-parity vector c [(Y-1) : 0] and the diagonal-parity vector d[max(X,Y) -1:0] (see also Fig. 24).

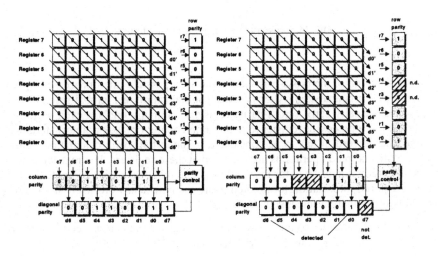

Fig. 24. Cross-Parity Organization for Register-Files

3.3.2 Cross-Parity Observation

For a concurrent error detection, respectively for an on-line check, a prediction logic for cross-parity (CPP = Cross-Parity Prediction) vectors has to be developed and implemented. According to the illustration in Fig.25, the principle should serve the on-line observation of register-file contents. The 'real' cross-parity (input from register output) will be permanently compared with the 'predicted' cross-parity (CPP) (actualized at the time of write signals according IC-signals or register input busses).

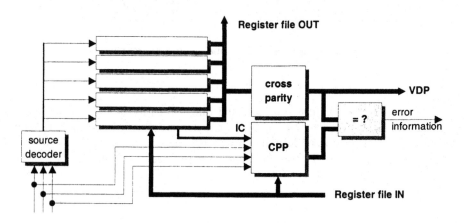

Fig. 25. Cross-Parity Observation structure

For the explanation of the cross-parity observation, a possible microprocessor register file (like Fig. 25) is analyzed. After processor initialization or a global reset, all registers contain usually zeros (cross-parity registers – initially one's = even parities of zero vectors). If a processor register (e.g. program counter or stack pointer) starts with an initial binary word, it has to be considered in the initial parity calculation. Subsequently, write and read operations are executed at these registers. If a register is written, special prediction circuits for row- column- and diagonal-parity compute updated parities. Required information for prediction are the new data word itself and the register address (destination select signals).

With bit width Y and the count of registers X, a register file can be seen as a matrix $M_{X,Y}$. The row-parity r_x can be calculated with a XOR/XNOR-junction of row-elements:

$$r_X = M_{X,Y-1} \oplus/\odot M_{X,Y-2} \oplus/\odot M_{X,Y-3} \oplus/\odot \ldots \oplus/\odot M_{X,0}$$

The prediction of row-parity can be carried out with the following logic circuits in Fig. 26. If a register is written, the complete row-parity has to be updated.

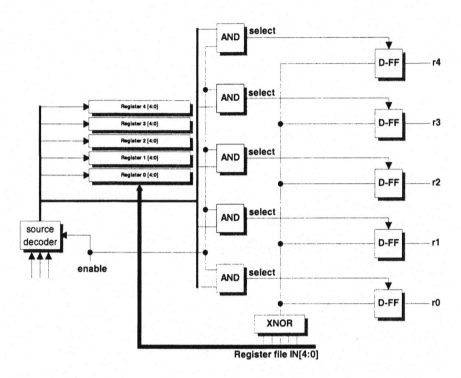

Fig. 26. Row-Parity Prediction Structure

The second element of cross-parity – the column-parity c_Y – can be ascertained with XOR/XNOR-junction of column elements:

$$c_Y = M_{X-1,Y} \oplus/\odot M_{X-2,Y} \oplus/\odot M_{X-3,Y} \oplus/\odot \ldots \oplus/\odot M_{0,Y}$$

For prediction of column-parity, it is inevitable to use internal signals of the register-file. Column-parity is changed at the time of register-writing, if the binary value of the according flip-flop is changed. Therefore, an *internal-change identification signal* IC was introduced. A new library element for the extended flip-flop with each two additional gates (XOR, AND) was created. The magnifying glass in Fig. 27 illustrates the changed flip-flop-type and the principle of the whole column-parity prediction. Accordingly, in column-parity prediction the complete vector has to be updated here, because a new register content may change all column-parity values. New parities are calculated with a setting of a T-flip-flop (T-FF) by an IC-signal from the selected column-element.

The changed register can be described with the following VHDL source code:

```
LIBRARY IEEE;
USE IEEE.std_logic_1164.ALL;

ENTITY icreg IS

   GENERIC (bits : integer);
   PORT    (
           clk  : IN bit;
           load  : IN bit;
           din  : IN bit_VECTOR(bits-1 DOWNTO 0);
           dout   : BUFFER bit_VECTOR(bits-1 DOWNTO 0);
           icvector : OUT bit_VECTOR(bits-1 DOWNTO 0)
              );
   END icreg;

ARCHITECTURE behavioral OF icreg IS

BEGIN

 reg: PROCESS

 BEGIN
 WAIT UNTIL(clk'event AND clk = '1');
    IF (load = '1') THEN dout<=din;
    ELSE
       NULL;
    END IF;
 END PROCESS;

 ic: PROCESS(din, dout, load)

   BEGIN
   FOR i IN bits-1 DOWNTO 0 LOOP
      icvector(i) <= (din(i) XOR dout(i)) AND load;
   END LOOP;
 END PROCESS;

END behavioral;
```

The number of diagonal parities Z results from the maximum of X or Y, because all bit elements have to be allocated to one diagonal d_z. For the exemplary 5x5-bit-register file as shown before, the diagonal-parities (from bottom-left to down-right) can be calculated as follows:

$$d_{z=4} = M_{4,4} \oplus/\odot M_{3,3} \oplus/\odot M_{2,2} \oplus/\odot M_{1,1} \oplus/\odot M_{0,0}$$
$$d_{z=3} = M_{4,3} \oplus/\odot M_{3,2} \oplus/\odot M_{2,1} \oplus/\odot M_{1,0} \oplus/\odot M_{0,4}$$
$$d_{z=2} = M_{4,2} \oplus/\odot M_{3,1} \oplus/\odot M_{2,0} \oplus/\odot M_{1,4} \oplus/\odot M_{0,3}$$
$$d_{z=1} = M_{4,1} \oplus/\odot M_{3,0} \oplus/\odot M_{2,4} \oplus/\odot M_{1,3} \oplus/\odot M_{0,2}$$
$$d_{z=0} = M_{4,0} \oplus/\odot M_{3,4} \oplus/\odot M_{2,3} \oplus/\odot M_{1,2} \oplus/\odot M_{0,1}$$

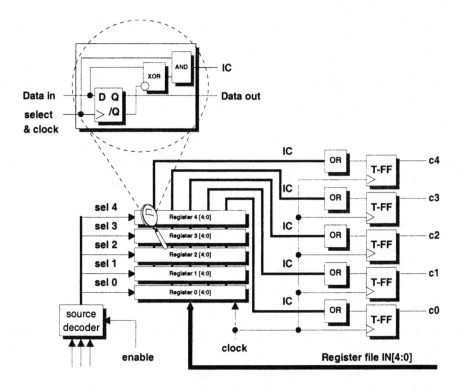

Fig. 27. Column-Parity Prediction Structure

For pre-calculation of the diagonal-parity the IC-signals has also to be considered. The scheme for prediction is outlined with the circuit shown in Fig. 28.

The following source code is the VHDL description of diagonal-parity prediction logic:

```
LIBRARY IEEE;
USE IEEE.std_logic_1164.ALL;

ENTITY diag_parity_pred IS
  GENERIC ( bits : integer;
               N : integer);
  PORT (
        reset : IN bit;   --synchronous reset
        clk   : IN bit;
        ic_vector : IN bit_vector((N*bits)-1 DOWNTO 0);
        diag_pred_vec : OUT bit_vector(bits-1 DOWNTO 0)
        );
END diag_parity_pred;
```

```
ARCHITECTURE behavioral OF diag_parity_pred IS
SIGNAL diag_sig : bit_vector (bits-1 DOWNTO 0);
SIGNAL diag_pred_sig : bit_vector (bits-1 DOWNTO 0);

BEGIN
-- generate xor-trees for diagonals
diags : FOR i IN (bits-1) DOWNTO 0 generate
   p0   : PROCESS(ic_vector)
      VARIABLE temp: bit;
      BEGIN

-- diagonals from left-up to right down
      temp:=ic_vector((bits*(N-1))+i);
      FOR j IN N-2 DOWNTO 0 LOOP
      temp:=temp XOR ic_vector((bits*j)+((i-1-j)MOD
                                                bits));

      END LOOP;
      diag_sig(i)<=temp;
   END PROCESS;
END generate;


-- Initialization parity vector and prediction
p1 : PROCESS
BEGIN
   WAIT UNTIL (clk'event AND clk='1');
   FOR i IN (bits-1) DOWNTO 0 LOOP
      IF(reset='1')THEN
         diag_pred_sig(i)<='1';
      ELSIF(diag_sig(i)='1') THEN

-- toggle, if parity is changed
         diag_pred_sig(i)<=NOT diag_pred_sig(i);
      END IF;
   END LOOP;
END PROCESS;

-- assign prediction vector
diag_pred_vec<=diag_pred_sig;

END behavioural;
```

3.3.3 Cross-Parity Error Detection Capabilities and Limitations

The Cross-Parity observation has the capability for a *diagnosis*. The localization of a single or multiple register error is realizable with an interpretation of parity vectors. In some cases, the identification of faulty bit-positions is possible. The following examples should explain the basic approach for the diagnosis according Fig. 24. The detection of a single error (e.g. at bit-position $M_{3,4}$) is trivial:

$$M_{3,4} = [r_3\text{-det}] \ \& \ [c_4\text{-det}] \ \& \ [d_0\text{-det}]$$

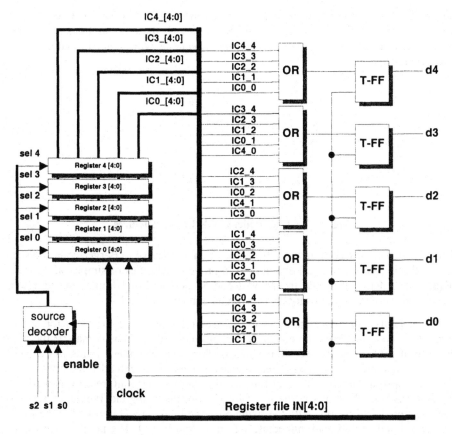

Fig. 28. Diagonal-Parity Prediction Structure

A double error in register 3 at bit-positions 4 and 5 is identified with the following logic equation.

$$M_{3,4/5} = [r_3\text{-not det}] \& [c_4\text{-det}] \& [c_5\text{-det}] \& [d_0\text{-det}] \& [d_1\text{-det}]$$

The identification of a quadruple error in register 3 and 4 at bit-position 4 and 5 is possible with the following equation:

$$M_{3/4,4/5} = [r_3\text{-not det}] \& [r_4\text{-not det}] \& [c_4\text{-not det}] \& \ldots \qquad \ldots$$
$$\& [c_5\text{-not det}] \& [d_7\text{-det}] \& [d_0\text{-not det}] \& [d_1\text{-det}]$$

This principle is easily transferable for various multiple error structure. Error condition "all bits inverted" in the register-file is undetectable with cross-parity observation, if the register bit width X is equal to the number of registers Y, and both (X, Y) are even (Fig. 29a). If moreover the bit-width is of type 2^n, a further multiple error structure is not detectable with cross-parity observation: if in all fault-affected rows, columns and diagonals the number of errors are even. An example is the 'chess-pattern' in Fig. 29b: all registers of every second diagonal are erroneous. Further examples are Fig. 31b and 31d. If otherwise the condition X≠Y is fulfilled and X or Y are odd respective X or Y are from type 2X–1 or 2Y–1, these possibilities are not existent. Then all faults (stuck-at, flip-to) are detectable with some limitations – as explained below.

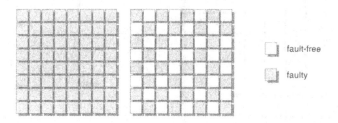

fault-free

faulty

Fig. 29. 'Logical'-undetectable Error structures

The cross-parity observation was introduced as an alternative to Berger-code registers in this thesis (see section 3.2) and also to improve capabilities of simple parity techniques. In order to illustrate the error detection potential and limitations of cross-parity observation, examples for register-faults will be discussed.

Classical fault-simulators regards in most cases only two fault locations for a flip-flop: at the data input line (D) and at the output line (Q). The reason may be the general use of ISCAS- or ISCAS-similar net-list format as example circuits. As a completion to this and with regards to real register-structures, an extended assumption for possible flip-flop faults at different functional modes (write, wait, read) was made. A condition is a stable signal at the input line before the rising clock edge of a rising edge triggered D-flip-flop. With the rising edge the input data D is stored in the internal state S and can be read immediately from output line Q. The point of view contains here furthermore a clock-line and a RST-line for the initialization or an asynchronous reset. As faults at D and Q, faults at these lines and a possible unexpected change of the register content due to a bit-flip must be considered. Fig. 30 illustrates assumed fault models.

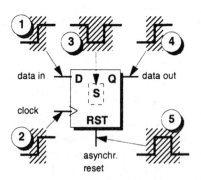

Fig. 30. Assumed Register Faults

1.   Transient faults at 'data in' lines particular at the time interval of a rising edge can lead to a storage of wrong data.
2.   Missing, premature or delayed clock signal due to a fault can also impede to take over the correct data.
3.   If a register is not written for many cycles, the internal state can change e.g. due to a bit-flip fault. The correct data is lost in this case. (This kind of error is a special example for a latent error.)
4.   Transient faults at the output line can lead to an unstable signal and with this to a wrong storage in the next sequential stage.
5.   Unforced reset- respective clear-signals due to faults at this lines destroy register contents.

Ref. 1.: Limitations for this fault model are given with bit-flip fault at the time of rising edge. A special fault-event is undetectable with CPP: Because of the access to register input and output signals (in order to generate *internal-change identification signal IC*, see also Fig. 27), even-multiplicity errors or 'symmetric' bit-flips in 2N flip-flops are undetectable during the write phase or the rising-edge of processor clock (Fig. 30). The reason is obviously the direct comparison (XOR) of new and previous flip-flop content. Table 6 explains the according constellations. Column D shows the actual data, which should be actual stored. Flip-to-0/1 (ft0/1) represents the assumed transient fault exactly during the rising edge. S_t and S_{t+1} are variables for the flip-flop state and the following state. The signal T is equal to the control signal of the column/diagonal-parity toggle-flip-flop (T-FF). A hook in column T and P represents a change of T-FF content respective of parity. According to Fig. 27, T represents the XOR-junction of register output and input – respective the value of bit-flip fault, because the toggle-flip-flop is controlled with the same rising edge. P shows the change in the real column/diagonal-parity. If T and P are changed at the same time, an observation of a fault is impossible. If a fault (e.g. bit-flip) occurred at data-in-line during the rising edge, the T-flip-flop of column- or diagonal-vector-element stores the wrong parity. For these special cases, only row-parity observation can be used for reliable error detection, but with known borders of error coverage (Fig. 31).

Table 6. Limitations for 'Data In' Line-Faults and Rising Clock Edge

ft-X	D	S_t	S_{t+1}	T	P	comment
0	0	0	0	-	-	Overwritten fault
0	0	1	0	✓	✓	Overwritten fault
0	1	0	0	-	-	Fault not detected
0	1	1	0	✓	✓	Fault not detected
1	0	0	1	✓	✓	Fault not detected
1	0	1	1	-	-	Fault not detected
1	1	0	1	✓	✓	Overwritten fault
1	1	1	1	-	-	Overwritten fault

flip-to-0

Ref. 2.: A transient fault at the clock line is obvious critical for the time of data storing. If the clock signal is active too early, the input signal may be not stable. For (low-power) designs with gated clocks, this fault assumption can model a missed rising clock-edge. For full-synchronous designs with independent clock and feedback of register content to the input over multiplexers, this model can represent faults at multiplexer-control lines. For this explanation, only a ft-0 is assumed. It represents a disturbed or missed clock edge.

Table 7. Examples for Clock-Line Faults

ft-X	D	S_t	S_{t+1}	T	P	Comment
0	0	0	0	-	-	Overwritten
0	0	1	1	✓	-	Detect
0	1	0	0	✓	-	Detect
0	1	1	1	-	-	Overwritten

Ref. 3.: This model should cover faults in registers between write-events. A flip-flop state can be changed due to a transient effect. The changed value is preserved. If a fault occurs but the content is not changed, than the error is from type *overwritten*. The cross-parity observation is suitably for this kind of possible latent errors. For flip-flops with gated clocks, the internal state S is regarded. In full-synchronous designs, this model can represent also faults at feedback-lines and/or multiplexers. A fault-forced change in control-vectors takes place here in Cross-parity vectors for the real register output. Predicted Cross-parity vectors are not toggled, because the AND-gate (see also Fig. 27) closes the internal change signal of the XOR-gate due to the missing enable signal (= select & clock). That leads to the statement: If a register is not written, all internal changes can be detected.

Table 8. Examples for Internal state Faults

ft-X	S_t	S_{t+1}	T	P	comment
0	0	0	-	-	overwritten
1	0	1	-	✓	detect
0	1	0	-	✓	detect
1	1	1	-	-	overwritten

Ref. 4.: In contrast to previous, this fault model represents momentary changes at the flip-flop output line (Q) during the rising edge of clock signal in spite of a correct data storage. It may lead to an unstable signal, from this it may follow a falsified data storage in the next register. A limitation for the detection of this type is equal to type 1. The error detection capability is limited to row-parity observation in case of faults in rows 2, 3, 6 and 7 of table 9. Multiple error structures like illustrations in Fig. 31 are not detectable.

Table 9. Limitations at Register 'Data Out' Lines

D	S_{t+1}	ft-X	Q	T	P	comment
0	0	0	0	-	-	overwritten fault
0	0	1	1	✓	✓	fault not detected
0	1	0	0	✓	✓	fault not detected
0	1	1	1	-	-	overwritten fault
1	0	0	0	-	-	overwritten fault
1	0	1	1	✓	✓	fault not detected
1	1	0	0	✓	✓	fault not detected
1	1	1	1	-	-	overwritten fault

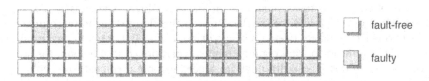

| | fault-free |
| | faulty |

Fig. 31. Examples for 'Rising-Edge'-undetectable Errors

Ref. 5.: A fault at the flip-flop RST line must be regarded, because a transient fault may lead to clearing of register content. To explain the capability of cross-parity observation for this fault model, a time interval from one rising edge to the next is considered. In a write cycle, a data at the input line (D), which should overwrite the previous stored data (S) leads in a fault-free case to D = S_{t+1}. A global reset signal is low-active in most cases of digital designs. Therefore, a flip-to-zero fault is considered. The constellation D = 1 S_t = 1 and a ft-0 fault (symmetric 2^{nv} ft-0 faults) exactly at the rising edge can not be detected (table 10: column 4). In the non-write mode, all fault of this time can be detected.

Table 10. Limitations for RST (ft-0) Faults in the Write Mode

D	S_t	ft-X	S_{t+1}	T	P	Comment
0	0	0	0	-	-	Overwritten
0	1	0	0	-	-	Overwritten
1	0	0	0	✓	-	Detect
1	1	0	0	✓	✓	not detect

For the case of changing of registers or register-cells in a non-write mode, the cross-parity is an excellent solution for an immediate error detection.

The CPP is also applicable to on-line observation of other processor registers beyond register files. According to the exemplary control-path in Fig. 15, registers can be disposed as a register-file for observation. For small processors, one Cross-Parity-controller is sufficient. For more complex systems with a greater part of registers and latches, a partitioning of observation is reasonable. In order to avoid long wires along the chip area, the register observation with CPP can be partitioned into several rasters according to the physical positioning of registers.

The suitability of cross-parity observation should also be investigated for memory structures like caches, ROM, PROM, EEPROM or RAM.

3.3.4 Results

Table 11 shows the necessary hardware costs for the Cross-Parity calculation and the prediction logic for exemplary register-files with various bit-length and register count. The actual vectors for Cross-Parity of the register-file contents is calculated with a direct access to register outputs. The gate count for prediction circuits is separately outlined for row-, column- and diagonal-parity vectors. Observation gate counts consider the sum of all circuits for the complete on-line check logic. The register-file itself, the decoder/address-logic and the overhead due to flip-flop-extension (according to Fig. 27 - in order to generate internal-change-identification IC) are not considered in this table. The overhead for observation circuits is partitioned in the count for necessary gates and flip-flops. These flip-flops are needed to store predicted row-, column- and diagonal-parity. The comparison with the real cross-parity is carried out with every rising clock-signal.

The Synthesis was carried out with FPGA*Express*™3.5 with option "optimized for speed". The net-list was mapped on a standard logic library from Lattice-Semiconductor.

Table 11. Hardware costs for Cross Parity Observation

Circuit	8 Register	16 register	32 register
8-bit Cross-Parity calculation	24 gates	64 gates	112 gates
8-bit row-parity prediction	11 gates + 8 ff	19 gates + 16 ff	35 gates + 32 ff
8-bit column-parity prediction	33 gates + 8 ff	41 gates + 8 ff	65 gates + 8 ff
8-bit diagonal-parity prediction	33 gates + 8 ff	41 gates + 8 ff	65 gates + 8 ff
CPP vector comparator	30 gates	39 gates	59 gates
8-bit Σ Cross-Parity *gates*	131	204	336
Observation *flip-flops*	24	32	48
16-bit Cross-Parity calculation	56 gates	160 gates	256 gates
16-bit row-parity prediction	12 gates + 8 ff	20 gates+ 16 ff	36 gates + 32 ff
16-bit column-parity prediction	65 gates + 16 ff	81 gates + 16 ff	129 gates + 16 ff
16-bit diagonal-parity prediction	65 gates + 16 ff	81 gates + 16 ff	129 gates + 16 ff
CPP vector comparator	50 gates	59 gates	75 gates
16-bit Σ Cross-Parity *gates*	248	401	625
Observation *flip-flops*	40	48	64
32-bit Cross-Parity calculation	104 gates	272 gates	480 gates
32-bit row-parity prediction	15 gates + 8 ff	23 gates+ 16 ff	39 gates + 32 ff
32-bit column-parity pred.	129 gates + 32 ff	161 gates+ 32 ff	257 gates + 32 ff
32-bitdiagonal-parity pred.	129 gates + 32 ff	161 gates+ 32 ff	257 gates + 32 ff
CPP vector comparator	90 gates	99 gates	115 gates
32-bit Σ Cross-Parity *gates*	467	716	1148
Observation *flip-flops*	72	80	96

Because the cross-parity observation was proposed as an alternative, the following table shows a direct comparison of both observation strategies. Especially, the register count for the BCP-observation of large register-files has an unacceptable amount. The cross-parity observation is here the better solution.

Table 12. Overhead – Comparison for Register-file Observation by BCP and CPP

Register observation technique [bit width]	Register-file with 8 registers	Register-file with 16 registers	Register-file with 32 registers
BCP [8-bit] gates **BC-register flip-flops**	257 8x4-bit = 32	257 16x4-bit = 64	257 32x4-bit = 128
CPP [8-bit] gates **CPP-vectors flip-flops**	131 (8+8+8)-bit= 24	204 (16+8+8)-bit = 32	336 (32+8+8)-bit = 48
BCP [16-bit] gates **BC-register flip-flops**	507 8x5-bit = 40	507 16x5-bit = 80	507 32x5-bit = 160
CPP [16-bit] gates **CPP-vectors flip-flops**	248 8+16+16 = 40	401 3x16-bit = 48	625 32+16+16 = 64
BCP [32-bit] gates **BC-register flip-flops**	1007 8x6-bit = 48	1007 16x6-bit = 96	1007 32x6-bit = 192
CPP [32-bit] gates **CPP-vectors flip-flops**	467 8+32+32 = 72	716 16+32+32 = 80	1148 3x32-bit = 96

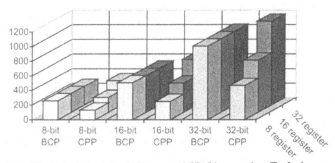

Fig. 32. Gate Count for BCP- and CPP Observation Techniques

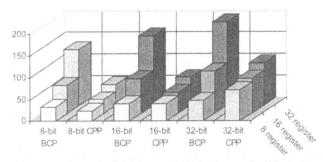

Fig. 33. Register Count for BCP- and CPP Observation Techniques

4. On-line Check Technology for Processor Control Signals

4.1 State of the Art

An obvious problem is the case of faulty control signals for fault-free components. Encoding and/or prediction techniques for component checks are useless if the wrong function is observed. Controller faults are to be seen in connection with an error latency. It leads often to exceptions, whereby the time of fault occurrence is rarely identifiable. Therefore, a large number of strategies was proposed for control flow check in processors. Mostly used techniques are based on *signature analysis* [61], [62], [35], [63]. For instance in [35], a special watchdog circuit is able to observe control flow signatures. Hellebrand and Wunderlich have proposed methods that perform controller error detection in the next clock cycle based on feedback shift registers and signature analysis [64]. These and similar techniques are in most cases combined with an error detection latency due to the analysis with shift registers. Because this delay doesn't allow fast recovering strategies like a micro-rollback, an on-line error detection within the same clock cycle is strongly necessary.

The simplest way for an online detection of arbitrary controller- respective control-signal errors is to duplicate - or for a fault-tolerant approach to triplicate the processor-FSM. The problem for such implementations is the possibility of identical errors in all modules caused by specification or synthesis faults. A more efficient alternative based on application-specific reduction of involved component is outlined in section 4.2 Furthermore, this principle guarantees a diverse implementation.

A recent approach for single fault detection is proposed in [65]: The controller-FSM of an embedded processor is split into tree distinct sub-machines. Authors proposed a decomposition into disjoint state machines to allow the generation of a control word and its duplicate within a checkpoint. (The meaning of a checkpoint is a set of time steps in this paper.)
An other possibility for control flow observation is given by using state encoding [66]. But for complex processors the check of processor states and according transitions is not realizable at reasonable cost. A more efficient starting point for on-line state machine observation is proposed in [20] and described in more detail in section 4.3.

4.2 Control-Signal On-line Check with Pseudo-TMR Controller

For the purpose of detecting arbitrary control logic errors in embedded processors, one possibility is to duplicate the control logic. A more efficient method is a form of pseudo-redundancy, which was proposed in [15].

Online error detection and correction by system implementation with triple-embedded processors and a voter circuit (Fig. 3), as in classical TMR fault-tolerant computing, is too expensive for most applications. The goal here was to achieve fault tolerance with a minimum of component redundancy. An advantage is that embedded processors run software that is known in advance. Thus, they don't need the "open" designs of general-purpose computers, which must run a great variety of software. A typical embedded system uses a general-purpose processor core with a large and complex instruction set ι_x. However, applications that run on an embedded processor usually require only a subset σ_y of instructions ($\sigma_y \subset \iota_x$). The basic concept is to provide a backup of just the control logic of the standard processor that is necessary for this instruction subset. As most embedded processors are based on CISC architectures, typically only a fraction of the actual instruction set is used. Then on-line test and eventually error compensation can also be limited to just this sub-set. This method increases the hardware overhead for redundant structures just by the necessary level.

The pseudo-TMR-principle plus a voter circuit for CL was implemented in order to make the control logic itself fault tolerant (Fig. 34). A decreasing hardware overhead of additional structures was achieved with the adoption to a given application, which runs on the processor (ADR = application-driven reduction). The basic idea was to observe only the correct activation of these control signals which are active during the actual application. Additional CL-units must generate only the necessary micro-instructions or control-signals according to the instruction sub-set of the given application. The advantage here was the fault-tolerant generation of micro-instructions and error detection at the same time.

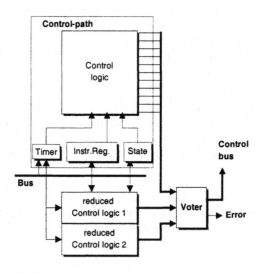

Fig. 34. Pseudo-TMR Control Logic

For a fast generation of a additional CL as a synthesiziable VHDL-file, the tool *cl_reducer* was developed. The following simple example and the according graphical representation in Fig. 35 outline the detailed algorithm for the CL-reduction. A set with two instructions is assumed:

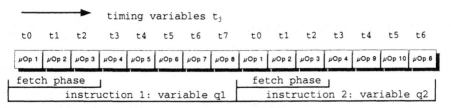

Fig. 35. Micro-operation sequence

To control the sequence of μOps, the following Boolean equations have to be synthesized as a control logic:

μOP1 = t0; μOP6 = t5 & q1 + t6 & q2;
μOP2 = t1; μOP7 = t6 & q1;
μOP3 = t2; μOP8 = t7 & q1;
μOP4 = t3 & (q1 + q2); μOP9 = t4 & q2;
μOP5 = t4 & q1; μOP10 = t5 & q2;

4.3 Control-Signal On-line Check with State Code Prediction

4.3.1 Introduction

In addition to various strategies for component on-line observation, the check of control signals has to be realized for a complete on-line error detection scheme – especial for embedded processors.

As a starting point for detecting control errors, an on-line technique is aspired in order to avoid any error latency potentially resulting in a failure.

The idea of the processor state machine observation was inspired by shortcomings of instruction set simulators: Various tools are able to emulate in detail the behavior of different processor types. They allow the representation of internal registers, memory content and actual execution steps. A detailed information about internal signals is rarely given, but is strongly needed to find bugs during the validation of new processor designs or newly implemented instructions. A traced control flow and the comparison with specified instruction set would allow a fast validation of implemented control logic.

Next step was the search for a possibility of an on-line error detection within the control flow in a real processor design – using the access to control lines. *Fast* on-line check is a pre-condition for strategies of fault compensation by processor backup or micro-rollback (see also chapter 5) without reset, halt or program-reloading. (Fast processor recovery strategies are urgently required for cores in safety-critical and/or real-time systems.)

The signature analysis strategy is unsuitable for on-line issues because of the latency problem of shift-registers. According to prediction techniques e.g. outlined for error detection in DP components (see also section above), a strategy was needed to check the actual control word by comparison with a second one, generated independently from the actual control path.

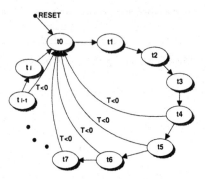

Fig. 36. Processor Timer / Sequencer Example

4.3.2 Straightforward Processor State Encoding and Observation

First, terms have to be defined which will be used in this approach. A *micro-operation* (μOp) or *micro-instruction* is associated with control signal(s) within the processor. An example is the control bits to load or to enable a register. A μOp serves to execute e.g. a register transfer operation within the same cycle. Letters $y_{0..x}$ are used as variables for μOps.

Micro-operations for data-path operations are usually assembled in a control-word $CW_{0..y}$ to address sources, destination and function for data manipulation. A sequence of μOps within a defined amount of cycles ($t_{0..i}$) (Fig. 35) is a *macro-instruction*. A fixed sequence of μOps is stipulated for every macro-instruction. The set of different macro-instructions is known as the instruction set of a processor. Simultaneously executed micro-operations at the time t_i are considered as a representation of the present *processor state*. The control logic (hardwired or micro-programmed) generates micro-operations y_x dependent on the op-code, on time-signals and on condition-flags.

The following example outlines this terminology. An common instruction for a procedure call in assembler language is the direct-addressed instruction CALL adr (Table 13). The instruction is fetched (t0 – t2) and decoded (q205). From t3 to t6 the target address is fetched. Within t7 to t11 the program counter's content as the return address is saved to the stack. The buffered jump address is loaded in the PC. Within the next fetch phase, the processor jumps to the new address and reads the first instruction of the procedure.

Less or more μOps can be executed concurrently according to the register independence. The grade of parallelism depends on the processor architecture [39] (see also section 2.2.2). Recurring y-vectors in all instruction sequences are defined in this thesis as a processor state S.

Table 13. μOp-Sequence Table for a CALL instruction

Instruc-tion	Conditions		Micro-Operations	Assigned Variables	Ass. States
Fetch	t0		MAR<-PC	Y0	S1
	t1		MBR<-M, PC<-PC+1	Y1, Y2	S2
	t2		IR<-MBR	Y3	S3
CALL	q205	t3	/QE_D, MAR<-PC	Y4, Y0	S69
adr	q205	t4	/QE_D, MBRL<-M, PC<-PC+1	Y4, Y17, Y2	S71
	q205	t5	/QE_D, MAR<-PC	Y4, Y0	S69
(Op-	q205	t6	/QE_D, MBRH<-M, PC<-PC+1	Y4, Y19, Y2	S72
code =	q205	t7	/QE_D, SP<-SP-1, INP<-MBR	Y4, Y83, Y18	S186
CD)	q205	t8	/QE_D, MAR<-SP, MBR<-PC	Y4, Y84, Y161	S187
	q205	t9	/QE_D, M<-MBRL, SP<-SP-1	Y4, Y9, Y83	S89
	q205	t10	/QE_D, MAR<-SP, OUT<-INP	Y4, Y84, Y162	S188
	q205	t11	/QE_D, M<-MBRH	Y4, Y11	S10
	q205	t12	/QE_D, MBR<-OUT	Y4, Y8	S7
	q205	t13	/QE_D, PC<-MBR	Y4, Y160	S185
	q205	t14	T<-0	Y12	S11

Real processor states S_{VCP1} are here defined exclusively as functions of simultaneously executed micro-instructions:

$$S_{VCP1} = f(y_x)$$

To involve signals of the control word for data-path components into the observation, the encoder has to be extended accordingly.

$$S_{VCP1} = f(y_x, CW_y)$$

The processor state machine can be looked at as a system which corresponds to a *zero order* Markov model [67]. In a *first order* Markov model the state at time $t+1$ only depends on the state at time t. If a state at time $t+1$ is independent of the previous state at time t, then the state machine corresponds to a Markov model of *zero order*.

For a prediction of the present state code needed for the comparison with the real code, conditions for control signal activation were included into the investigation. The actual state is represented by the simultaneously active control signals. The expected state code S_{VCP2} is generated with the CSP(Control-Signal-Prediction)-unit at the same time with S_{VCP1}.

$$S_{VCP2} = f(t_i, q_k, c_l);$$

$i \in [0..\text{maximum time for one instruction}];$

$k \in [0..\text{instruction set length}];$

$l \in [0..\text{flag-signal count}]$

Proprietary processor design are shortly described in the appendix.

To by-pass the control logic, conditions for control-flow sequences were used. The first variable is the instruction q_k, which is obtained from a direct access to the memory/cache/pre-fetch-unit output-bus. The op-code is read from CSP at the time it is on the bus. The time variable t_i, which controls the μOp-sequence, sets the second condition. Through an original timer- or sequencer or through an optional second timer, time variables t_i are accessible. Because of the common existence of conditional instructions (e.g. branch if zero), flag-signals have to be included e.g. from condition code registers into our prediction unit. Conditions or flag signals c_i (e.g. carry, sign, zero, overflow, interrupt-flags, etc.) are also fed to the CSP-unit (Fig. 37).

Table 14. Instruction-, μOp-sets and State-Spaces of Various Processor Designs

Design	Instructions	Micro-instr.	$\varnothing$ CPI	Legal States
t4008*	61	56	8.98	67
t5008m	210	190	7.28	187
t5016	204	181	7.57	170
t5016m	214	193	7.49	189
t5016mp	214	193	14.00	103**
SRC32	32	77	22.16	106
t5032	202	133	6.29	176
t5032m	212	145	6.13	185
UDSP32a	45	49	5.27	43
UDSP32b	70	84	5.74	92
U320C20-d	60	48	5.75	57
DLX64p_fpu*	32	41	3.80	148**

(d ... derivative, *... 3-address machine, **... partitioned state spaces for pipeline-stages)

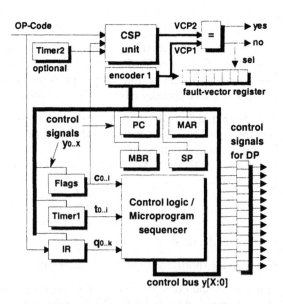

Fig. 37. Structure of State code comparison

With the assumption of permanent or transient faults within the control logic, at control lines, or in control registers, the following possible erroneous processor behavior should be detected:

- One or more necessary μOps are inactive, which may leave the macro-instruction executed in parts only
- One or more μOps, which are normally inactive, become active, which may cause an overwriting of important data (e.g. instruction- or address-code)
- Combination of the two conditions above

To encode all possible states derived from these points, all possible sets of control signals, respectively all possible combinations of μOps, have to be regarded. The following example calculates the number of states (legal plus illegal) for a proprietary 16-bit processor (t5016) with 214 instruction, whose instruction set is similar to Intel's 8085/86 (see also Appendix). The processor has 193 different micro-instructions. Under the restrictive assumption of at maximum 10 simultaneously active μOps, the following count of states was reached:

$$\sum_{i=0}^{10} C_{193}^{(i)} = \sum_{i=0}^{10} \frac{193}{i!(193-i)} = 1.648034747 \cdot 10^{16} \quad \text{states.}$$

If only a maximum of 5 simultaneously active micro-instructions is assumed, the calculation still results in:

$$\sum_{i=0}^{5} C_{193}^{(i)} = \sum_{i=0}^{5} \frac{193}{i!(193-i)} = 2,175,230,626 \quad \text{states.}$$

Here 32 bits are necessary to encode the state space completely. Therefore and because of the aspired comparison with a predicted state code, we encode only legal states. Legal states are derived from the real macro-instruction set and the respective μOps. Table 14 gives an overview of some implemented processors with their respective macro- and micro-operations and the number of legal states. To keep the pure combinatorial character needed for on-line test, transitions between states are not observed.

The principle – to encode only legal states – involves a further problem: In case of an illegal state, encoder 1 produces a zero-vector for VCP1. A fault-classification after a micro-rollback (see chapter 5.) is no longer possible, because this vector should be used for an error-recognition. To circumvent this identification problem, it is possible to store the micro-instructions – belonging to an illegal state. If a micro-rollback is planned, an error (VCP1 = '000...000') can be (firstly) assumed, caused by a transient fault-event. After a defined amount of rollback-operations with a recurrent error detection, a permanent fault must be assumed. For a later fault-analysis or for a fault-reconstruction, the predicted state-code VCP2 for the according time can be saved.

To investigate this strategy for on-line state machine observation, check units for different processor architectures (see also Table 15) were implemented with different complexities. It was first assumed that embedded systems or SOCs contain a CISC-type processor core. With the help of different instruction- or μOp-sets, the suitability of our concept for an on-line control-flow check was validated. VHDL-files for encoders and CSP-units for all soft-cores were generated and synthesized. The overhead for the complete state machine observation unit is about 70% to 90% for processors with a small gate count and small instruction sets (e.g. for t4008=1232 Gates, 67 in-structions we reach 74% overhead). For processors with larger gate counts and in-struction sets, the overhead is almost 25% because of a higher share of equal states in different control-flow-sequences (e.g. for t5032m=9677 Gates, 212 instructions we reached 24,2% overhead).

Table 15. CSP-Overhead for 'sequential' Processors

Design *3-address machines	Instr. Set	Gate count	Overhead (gates)
t4008	61	1232	74.2 %
t5016	204	2566	96.1 %
t5016m	214	4524	63.8 %
t5032	202	7954	29.0 %
t5032m	212	9677	24.2 %
uDSP32a	45	27621	2.4 %
uDSP32b	70	57442	2.1 %
U320C20-d	60	8995	7.4 %

The basic gate count for check units (VCP1-encoder, CSP and comparator) grows up to a relatively fixed level for every core and changes only slightly in case of addition-ally implemented instructions (if for relative flexible functionality a *minimum-necessary* instruction set already exists). The reason is that new micro-operation se-quences can mostly be built with already existing states.

4.3.3 Partitioned State Encoding and Observation

Beyond simple processors with fixed-length instruction sequences, state machines of pipelined, super-scalar and/or MIMD-processors are much more complex. With the help of a proprietary pipelined processor-design, the suitability of the approach was basically validated also for such architectures.

In processors with instruction look-ahead operations or in common pipeline proces-sors [39], the complexity of the control-flow grows rapidly. The basic principle of a pipeline without hazards is outlined in Figure 38. Five stages are assumed here: In-struction Fetch (IF), Instruction Decode and Register Fetch (ID), Execution and Ad-dress Calculation (EXE), Memory Access (MEM) and Write back (WB) [39].

A pre-calculation of the overhead in case of an encoding of all possible simultane-ously active control signals during all time steps (Fig. 39) produces a too-large state space. For a pipelined operation without hazards, 123840 legal states were calculated. The state encoder and the prediction unit were modified therefore. Different encoders for every pipeline stage (Fig. 40) were implemented. Now different amounts of states for pipeline-stages were reached. The EXE-stage contains the maximum with 148 possible states.

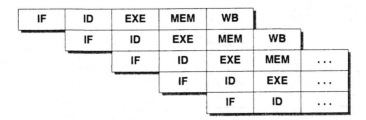

Fig. 38. Basic Pipeline principle

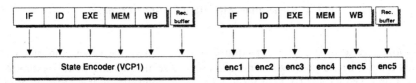

Fig. 39. State encoding Variant 1   **Fig. 40. State encoding Variant 2**

To show the applicability to processors with a higher complexity, check units for state machine on-line observation of a 32-bit and a 64-bit pipeline-microprocessor with super-scalar data-path and hardware-implemented hazard-control (DLX32p_fpu and DLX64p_fpu; for architecture description – see Appendix A) were designed. Through the partitioning of the on-line state observation unit to every pipeline stage, for the *complete modified* unit an overhead of 20,4% for the DLX32p_fpu was reached and only 5,8% for the DLX64p_fpu [20].

The reason is first the ratio 'large data-path ↔ small control-path', but a further reason is the partitioning into smaller on-line check units and the combination of their results into an efficient observation of the whole processor state machine.

A further possibility for an increasing efficiency of state code observation is given by the ADR-principle which was already used for control-logic reduction. This is applicable if standard processors with a relative complex instruction set use only a sub-set of instructions in embedded systems with a limited count of applications. Then an embedded processor, during its operation in a fault-free case, reaches only a part of all possible states. The algorithm in Fig. 41 outlines the basic principle.

The analysis of the application code is used for the extraction of the instruction sub-set – respective the μOp-sub-set. The next function parses the 'remaining' μOp-sequences and assigns state code variables. A user-defined classification of micro-operations allows a partitioning of the complete state encoder.

4.3.4 Outlook Regarding to Controller On-line Check

Controller structures – respective control-paths are the most critical part in a processor design. In contrast to data-path with mostly regular structures, standards for CPs are not existent.

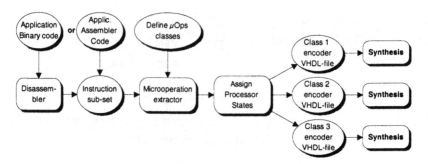

Fig. 41. Generation-Algorithm for State Encoders

A conjoint characteristic of every controller is obviously the generation of control-signals for the whole processor. This should be also the starting point for future investigations. The easiest strategy for a dependable controller is the TMR or pseudo-TMR. Straightforward state encoding and observation is preferable for processors with a non-complex architecture (possibly for some RISCs). For more complex structures, a partitioned processor state spaces and according encoders bring an acceptable overhead. Moreover, a reasonable partitioning has the basic capability for a diagnosis – respective for a (coarse-grained) error localization.

A current research project deals with a control-signal observation in order to identify erroneously controlled components. This is necessary, if different error-handling strategies can carried out according to the error weighting or priority (see also section 5.3). The observation principle bases on a comparison of control-words coming from two divers designed CL-components (identification of the Boolean difference). Differences may occur for single or multiple errors and will be processed by a priority controller, which initialized according error handling strategy or simultaneous strategies (Fig. 42).

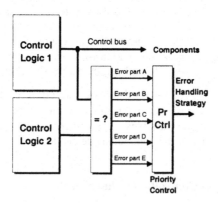

Fig. 42. Error Handling Priority Control

5. Fast Processor Recover Techniques with Micro Rollback

The precursory proposed techniques for on-line observation of processor components and signals was developed in order to detect errors within a single clock cycle. According to Fig. 16, this is a precaution to carry out a fast error handling procedure in order to avoid a functional error. In this thesis, the focus on a fast error detection and recovery is directed at embedded processor- or micro-controller-based applications with a highly safety-critical relevance or strong real-time constraints. Methods should have a high efficiency, that means the overhead should be significantly less than the silicon area for TMR or quadruple modular redundancy. Furthermore, different handling-strategies for different fault-classes (transient, permanent) are needed. A distinction between transient effects and permanent faults (of static or dynamic origin) is important, since only permanent faults need additional stand-by hardware for compensation.

5.1 Previous Techniques and State of the Art

Derived from simple error detection schemes with multiple modules, a recover or a repair strategy with multiple processors is easy implementable. A lot of industrial and academic examples for dependability for *re-configurable processor architectures* have been published in recent years.

The Stratus self-checking processor [68] is based on a "pair and spare" concept. The whole system is built by duplicating two paired CPUs. The fault-tolerant architecture of Stratus uses physically four CPUs to realize one logic CPU. The Sun ft-SPARC™ fault-tolerant platform [69] contains a fault-tolerant core, which consists of two processor / memory subsystems, each containing one to four SPARC-processors. The dual configuration provides continuous operation in the event of failure. Another approach concerns generic upgradeable architectures for real-time dependable systems [70]. The IBM S/390 processor [71] is used for high-end server applications – often as a multiple processor "mainframe". Processor cores are arranged in a matrix and can work in parallel. According to the custom demands, a defined count of processors within the "mainframe" is activated. If the customer needs a higher performance, other CPUs can be switched to an active mode via a combination of hardware and licensed internal code. In case of a hardware error, the previous status is recovered by replacing the erroneous CPU. The realization of conventional fault-tolerant processor designs is rather expensive for many applications. It is a great challenge for building dependable embedded systems to reduce the hardware-overhead of these solutions. For applications without multiple processors, techniques with a hybrid redundancy were proposed. From practical experience it can be assumed that a large number of transient faults can be repaired by repeating the operation in a controlled manner using the same hardware again [72]. Specially for non-permanent faults, the *rollback (RB) principle* is an efficient method for processor execution sequences. The RB-principle is basically a repetition of an erroneous operation outgoing from a defined (saved) *checkpoint* in the past. A checkpoint is commonly a defined "snapshot" of the state (e.g. start of an instruction sequence, start of a software-loop, etc.). The objective of classical RB-techniques is to restore the system state by overwriting the current state with a snapshot taken in the past (at the last passed checkpoint). Rollback is used in software-routines [73] as well as in sequential hardware [74]. The execution of interrupt-routines or an exception-handling in microprocessors can be seen as examples for RB. Here, processor-states (register contents) are rescued to the stack at defined time-points. If an error occurs within the next instruction sequences, processor-registers can be updated with saved register contents. General, RB is executable within the regular operation and is therewith predestinated for on-line recovering. A lot of RB-techniques use large time-intervals between checkpoints. In most applications, it is expected that errors are rare and large delays for recovery are acceptable. Checkpointing in such applications may be performed only once every few millions of cycles. Furthermore, recover-techniques are often software-controlled, hence the whole restoring process itself may take thousands of cycles. An objective of this thesis is the ability to detect errors as soon as they occur and start immediately with error handling strategies in order to prevent propagated errors throughout the whole system. A hardware mechanism for fast rollback of a few cycles is proposed by Tamir and Tremblay in [74]. The presented *micro-rollback* technique is able to recover a number of cycles. This *rollback-distance* is limited by the number of stored snapshots. In this paper, the maximum rollback-distance is the *rollback-range* which is dependent on the latency of the detection and correction mechanism.

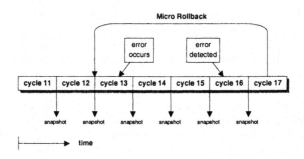

Fig. 43. Micro Rollback of a Module - Source: [74]

Tamir and Tremblay proposed micro-rollback-supported register-files. With a N-word FIFO (first-in first out) buffer, which is called as a delayed write buffer, the register contents can be restored in case of an error. Snapshots are only realized for register-files. Other processor registers are not considered. Furthermore, Tamir et al. proposed a scheme with self-checking   and self-repairing *mirror processors* in [75]. This scheme is built with two RISC processors. A concurrent error detection is achieved with a comparison of external signals A mismatch leads to a rollback to the last error-free cycle. In order to decrease the error detection latency for some transient single bit faults, a comparison of signatures of internal signals is introduced. For latent errors, a backup from the slave- to the master-mirror processor or vice versa is proposed. The determination, which processor has the correct value, is carried out with an additional single parity bit. The advantage of this approach is that a checkpointing and a "snapshot"-storing is not necessary. But a disadvantage is that the proposed handling for latent errors is only used for the case of an error occurrence in register-files. Furthermore, single parity check can only detect single bit errors or errors which have not a even multiplicity [76]. A presence of latency for error detection at external pins or the analysis of internal signatures is obvious. The error recovery in case of a permanent fault is not considered.

5.2 Micro Rollback with a Master-Trailer-Structure

With previously proposed techniques of an error detection within the same clock cycle, a faster micro rollback is possible. The implemented hardware structure consists of a primary processor – *the master* and a co-processor – *the trailer*. Master and trailer are equipped with built-in self-check facilities. A combination of control-signal-, Berger-code- and Cross-Parity-prediction is used. The trailer is clocked synchronously with the main processor and executes the same program with a delay of one clock cycle. This delay is easily realizable with a single-word FIFO at the input of the trailer. If the actual contents of all processor storage elements is seen as the present processor state, the trailer reaches the master-state one cycle later. Hence, the *rollback distance* is one cycle. This distance is customizable to other error detection techniques. The choice for such an architecture with master and trailer was taken, because a distinction between transient and permanent faults and the compensation of the first hardware error was aspired. A further advantage of a fast error detection and 'one cycle'-rollback distance is a possible repair before erroneous data can be re-written to the memory.

5.2.1 Micro Rollback Test Circuit

With the following example of a simple Accumulator/ALU circuit, the suitability of the micro-RB principle with a one cycle RB distance is validated. The test circuit (see also the schematic screen-shot in Fig. 44) contains an 8-bit ALU and two edge-triggered registers for buffering of operands A and B. The register for the operand A is the accumulator. It's inputs are connected to the ALU-outputs. A 4-bit register buffers control-signals (ALU_F[2:0], ALU_CIN) for the ALU.

For a first validation of the aspired micro RB principle, errors only in the accumulator-register and within the ALU are injected. For fault detection, the Berger-code prediction is used (see also section 3.2). The ALU can be observed by comparison of the predicted BC according to the selected function and the real BC of the result. The BC of a new accumulator-content is saved and will be check after the register is read.

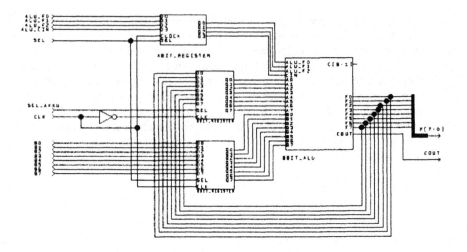

Fig. 44. Schematic of the Accumulator/ALU Test Circuit

The extended circuit (Fig. 45) contains as additional elements:

- a BCP-unit,
- a register for saving of the Berger-code of the accumulator-content,
- a BC-checker for the accumulator-content,
- a BC-checker for the ALU-result.

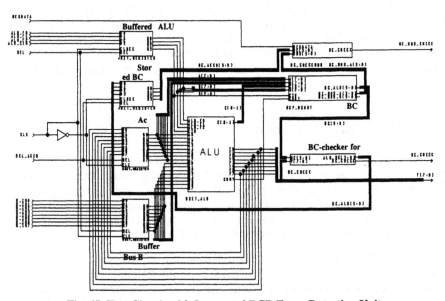

Fig. 45. Test Circuit with Integrated BCP-Error Detection Units

An error occurrence in the ALU is identified by a high-value at the output of the BC_CHECK component. Through a comparison of stored BC of the accumulator-content and the Berger-coded operator of the A-bus (A-input of the ALU), an error within the accumulator can be detected.

Remark: The overhead for the simple accu/ALU-circuit is really high, but is not considered in this case. For real data-paths in combination with register-files, the ratio is better.

After an error detection, a rollback-mechanism has to be started which restores the previous accumulator-content and repeats the operation. The previous accumulator-content can be stored with regular snapshots or with the proposed trailer-circuit. The following scheme in Fig. 46 shows the basic structure of the rollback-circuit with a master-trailer constellation. The trailer is first assumed as fault-free. The architecture is extended with the trailer circuit, with multiplexers and a rollback-controller.

In an error-free case, the master-accu stores the ALU result. In the case of a detected error, the *select*-signal stops the trailer and the master. The master-accu is updated by the trailer-accu trough the *MUX*. The master repeats the previously erroneous operation within the next cycle.

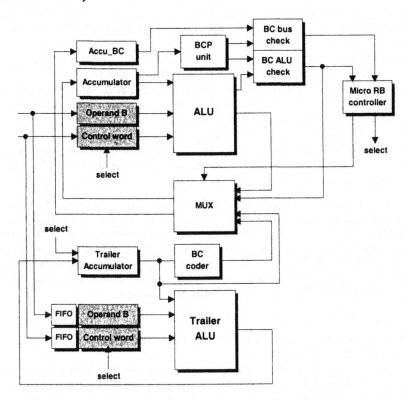

Fig. 46. Integrated BCP-Error Detection Units Block Diagram

The time diagram in Fig. 47 explains the necessary delay for the trailer circuit. Accumulator registers are *negative* edge triggered. The regular operation starts after a falling edge (400.0ns).

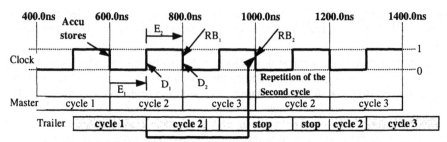

Fig. 47. Time Diagram of Micro RB for the Test Circuit

With the next rising edge of the clock, buffer-registers store the data for the control word and for the operand B. After this, results are at outputs of both ALUs and at the inputs of accu-registers. By the time of 600.0ns, accu-registers store new data. The detection of an error can be carried out immediately, but registration in a error-flag is only possible at the time of a falling or rising edge. If an error occurs at the interval E_1, the rollback can be started after the error-flag-setting at D_1. At this time, the possibly erroneous result of the ALU is not stored in the accu yet. If the error is caused by a transient effect with the duration of E_1, the error is of type *overwritten*. If the duration is longer than E_1 or if the error firstly occurs in E_2, the erroneous result of the ALU is stored with falling edge at D_2. As the accu-content is immediately present at the input of the ALU, the error can be propagated and leads to a faulty result, although no error is identified.

A rollback activation is possible at D_1 or D_2. A reasonable solution is the start of the rollback RB_1 at D_2, because the accumulator can only be distorted with the negative edge. Error flags are only stored at D_2. The maximum duration from the first error occurrence to the RB initialization is limited to one cycle. The restoring of the accu-content needs a further cycle. With this, the recovery of an error caused by a transient fault (within one cycle) takes two cycles. From the time diagram in Fig. 47, it is obvious that the delay for the trailer must be only half a cycle.

5.2.2 Micro Rollback Technique for Simple Microprocessors

A rollback scheme for a whole processor core can be derived from the test circuit in principle as outlined before. But it has to consider higher complexity of the state which has to be recovered. As in the example above, in [74] and in [75], the rollback mechanism is limited to registers in data-paths or to register-files. In microprocessors, a state is represented with the actual contents of all data- and control-registers. As in a sequence of micro-operations (μOps), register-contents can be changed in every cycle, the micro rollback with a distance of one cycle is a very good solution for recovery in case of transient effects. Especially for branch- or jump-instructions with a 'radical' change of the processor state, fast error detection and recovery is a must. To take snapshots of all registers in every cycle is too expensive in terms of the needed storage hardware and power consumption. The better solution is given with two processors as the master-trailer scheme [19]. With the proposed delay of one cycle, the master state is present one cycle longer in the trailer.

With the assumption that errors in components and control-signal errors are detectable in the whole processor device, the master is equipped with built-in self-check (BISC) units. The trailer is first assumed as fault-free. The master-trailer scheme was implemented in such a way that within the rollback-mode an update of register contents from one to the other processor (here firstly: trailer→master) is possible. That implies additional multiplexers, lines and busses and with this also additional critical paths may be possible, if macro-blocks for master and trailer are implemented separately. This problem can be circumvented or at least extenuated with an intermixed design of both processor cores (e.g. both register-files are located directly abreast on the chip). For an explanation of the proposed principle, separate processors are illustrated.

The structure of the micro rollback top-design is shown in Fig. 48. The principle of the BISC units is explained in chapter 3 and 4. The location of the rollback controller is not inevitably prescribed, but may be adopted to timing constraints of eventual critical paths.

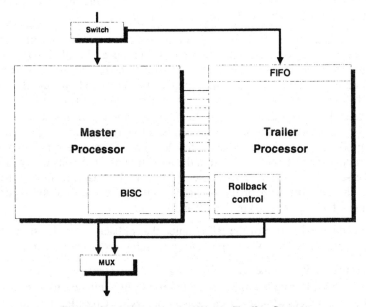

Fig. 48. Basic Scheme of a Master-Trailer-Structure

The time-delayed operation of the trailer is reached by an one-word FIFO. The master-processor (and finally also the trailer) is equipped with additional logic for every register or latch. The input of every storage element comes from a multiplexer which leads through the real input from the according bus or the input from the corresponding trailer-register within the rollback mode. After a detected error and the initialization of the rollback, all registers/latches are reloaded with contents before the error occurrence. During the repetition of the erroneous cycle, the trailer waits.

The basic idea for an intelligent fault handling - respective an intelligent error recovery - starts from the (positive) assumption that the error is caused by a transient effect within one cycle (single-event upset). After the recovery, it must be checked if the fault was really transient. Otherwise a permanent fault (e.g. a physical defect) has to be assumed. In this case the trailer takes over the complete functionality of the master, which can be tested or repaired off-line. In practical applications it can be assumed that, after the trailer processor alone supports a system function, a maintenance and repair action is called for at the next convenient time. Such a level of fault-tolerance is quite reasonable for many applications e. g. in the automotive area. This micro rollback strategy will be discussed with the following steps:

- **Rollback mode** <= an error is detected: stop master and trailer operations and start rollback
- **Micro rollback**: load all trailer register-contents into according master components
- **Retry** the previous faulty cycle in the master and observe the correct operation
- **Continued operation** <= no error is detected (Fig. 49); trailer continues with one cycle delay
- **Switch mode** <= the same error is detected (Fig. 50): hand over the operation to the trailer (and start offline test of the faulty master)

In order to characterize the fault-event as a transient effect or a permanent fault, the rollback-controller observes special fault vectors – produced by BISC-units. As outlined in chapter 3 and 4, BISC-principles are based on special encoding strategies. The proposed BISC-units produce always predicted and real code words (BC-, Cross-Parity- and state-code). For an identification of a recurred fault, the respective *real codes* are used if an 'error-detect'-flag is set. This sanction to use this code as a representation for a fault was made, because it can be strongly assumed that the encoding hardware produces the same fault-vector for the same recurring error. It is very unlikely that a new and different fault within the repetition of a previous faulty cycle can produce the same fault vector. In this case, the new fault is handled first as a permanent fault. The time-behavior of the proposed strategy for the handling of transient and permanent faults is outlined in Fig. 49 and Fig. 50.

If an error is detected in one of the BISC-units, the rollback controller stores the according fault-vector(s). The following fault-representing vectors are possible:

- **Vector VDP** from the ALU-observing BCP-unit (see also Fig. 17)
- **Vector VDP** from the register-file-observing BC-unit (see also Fig. 18)
- **Vector(s) Cross-Parity** from register-observing Cross-Parity-unit (see also Fig. 25)
- *Vector VCP1 = 0 (for legal-states encoder) from state-code-observing unit (see also Fig. 35)*

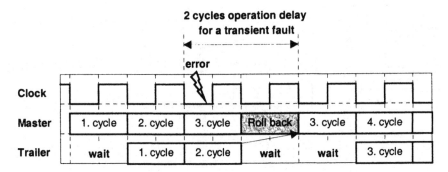

Fig. 49. Duration for Transient Fault Handling

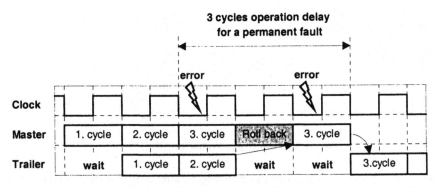

Fig. 50. Duration for Permanent Fault Handling

Remark: In point four, the storage of predicted state-code VCP2 can be carried out for the fault-event reconstruction within an off-line test. The reason is the state-encoding of only legal states. If, due to a fault, an illegal error is reached, vector VCP1 is equal to zero. An alternative is to store μOp-signals of the current step for an identification of a recurrent fault or to identify the difference of two divers implemented CL-components (see section 4.3.4).

The following Fig. 51 shows a screenshot of a rollback-controller for an 8-bit demon-stration processor (t4008). In this example, fault-vector comparisons according to points 1, 2 and 4 are implemented.

An error is detected here, if one of the comparators detects a difference between the respective code-vectors. A *master-slave-slave* D-flip-flop (S1, S2, S3) is used for the error signal within a rollback mode. With this error in the cycle i, the respective fault-vector in the cycle i+1 is stored (V1) and the first D-FF (S1) is set. The rollback is initiated. With the next falling edge of clock, S2 is set and the trailer is stopped. The next rising edge in cycle i+2 is used for the rollback, and the shift of fault-vector into the next register (V2). After the repeated master-operation (cycle i+3), fault-vectors will be compared. The time-scheme in Fig. 52 outlines this flow.

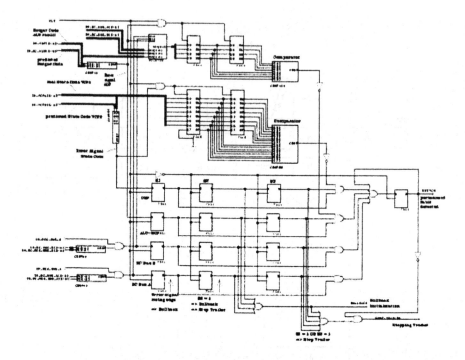

Fig. 51. Schematic of a Rollback-Controller

So far, a transient effect within one cycle (during or after a rising edge) is assumed. If the model of a transient fault (e.g. flip-to-0/1) is extended to a duration of more than one cycle, the rollback controller can easily be adapted: After rollback cycle and repetition of erroneous cycle, an iterated fault with the same fault vector is not instantly considered as a permanent fault. For instance, a transient fault is defined with a maximum duration of two cycles. The rollback is initiated twice. If after this the fault is still present, it can be handled as a permanent effect.

5.2.3 Results

The overhead for an architecture with a self-checking master and a (self-checking) trailer plus the rollback-controller is obviously higher than a simple duplication. In experiments with example processors with a sequential micro-instruction flow (see also Appendix), the gate count of the implemented structure is in most cases less than TMR plus voting circuits schemes. For instance, the 8-bit processor-design t4008 has a basic gate count of 1421. The master-design with self-check (BCP, CSP) and rollback (multiplexors) facilities needs 3507 gate equivalents. The rollback-controller, the FIFO and further components need approximately 280 gates. A summarized expenditure for master plus (non-self-checking) trailer plus rollback-controller of 5208 can compete with a TMR plus voter scheme. For other example processors, the overhead is similar. An improvement can be reached with optimization of BISC-units, especially with partitioning of state-encoding units (see section 4.3.3) or with a tricky combination of component-BISC-units (BCP and CPP).

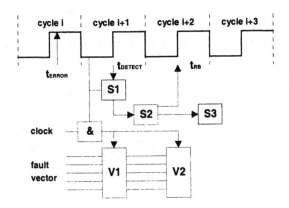

Fig. 52. Time Behavior of the Rollback Controller

For a completion of the proposed scheme for dependability, the trailer must also be implemented as a self-checking processor with rollback facilities. Then, the whole hardware expenditure increases to 6400 gate equivalents. A scheme with two self-checking processors is approximately identically to a quadruple-modular redundant processor (according the level of dependability), Therefore, the overhead is reasonable with regard to distinction and different handling of fault-classes.

5.3 Micro Rollback in Pipeline-Processors

For more complex processors (e.g. with pipelined or super-scalar μOp-flow, floating-point units, etc.), the micro rollback principle with a master and a trailer seems to be too expensive. But in such structures, the previous approach can be effectively implemented with the use and/or the negligible extension of internal structures.

5.3.1 Recover Techniques for a Pipeline Processor

In contrast to processors with a sequential μOp-flow, instructions are executed in parallel as in Fig. 36. A micro-rollback by repetition of erroneous cycle is in some cases impossible, because according components of the pipeline may execute the stage of the next instruction.

The easiest way to recover the pipeline-state after an error is to repeat the complete program. This corresponds to a reset and program-restart in common microprocessor- or controller-applications. A further uncomplicated possibility is to refill the complete pipeline. Therefore, the program-counters of every instruction must be stored, which was fetched into the pipeline. The pointer will be reloaded, which was in the write-back (WB) pipeline-phase if an error was detected. If WB consist of a NOP instruction, the pointer of instruction is loaded, which is in the MEM-phase (and so on). A technique with a shorter recover latency can be realized with a special processor mode: with double-fetching of an instruction into the pipeline (Fig. 53). If an error is detected, a stage-rollback can be carried out. For the handling of transient effects, this is a easy-implementable solution with performance degradation by a factor of 2.

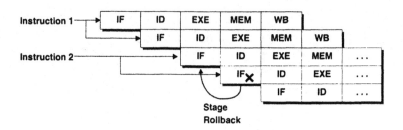

Fig. 53. Stage-Rollback in a Pipeline

A stage rollback is possible also without double fetching: Pipelining is based on data shifting from registers/latches to registers/latches of the next stage according to a processor clock. (The 'shifting' is certainly combined with a special operation.) A simple analogy is a 'creeping earthworm': The front of the worm is stretched, during the rear part holds out on the spot. After the front has arrived at the next point, the rear part is dragged afterwards. This means for a rollback facility in a pipelined processor that in case of an error within a stage ('to the next point stretched worm'), the cycle can be repeated ('the front of the earthworm flips back') due to held data. If 'start'-registers of according stage are not yet overwritten from previous registers, a rollback to 't0' of this stage is realizable with changed pipeline control but no additional hardware. This strategy is suitable especially for pipeline-stages with a multicycle execution. If the internal structure of pipeline processors doesn't allow this efficient stage-rollback (especially in stages with a short execution time), a simple extension of the register-structure can be implemented. The simplest way to protect stage-'start'-registers from overwriting is a FIFO-structure. A further possibility is offered by additional inverse triggered registers. The following basic structure (Fig. 54) illustrate the principle.

A second 'remember'-register Rx' is included which stores data at the falling edge (inverse triggered). If an error is detected within this cycle, a multiplexer switches saved data in the stage for a repetition of operation. This extension is suitable for a rollback in short stages. Obvious problems are given with critical paths due to additional components of the *design-for-rollback*. In most cases Rx'-registers and multiplexers are not necessary. Rather, if the pipeline timing allows it, an adaptation of the pipeline-controller is sufficient, in order to hold longer contents of pipeline stage 'start'-registers.

The logic- and register-structure in a pipeline itself can often be used for a micro-rollback. In consideration of appropriate on-line check facilities, a micro-rollback with an one-cycle delay is feasible by re-generation of according controll-signals.

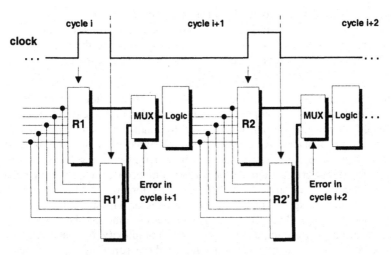

Fig. 54. Pipeline with Rollback Facility

The overall concept to repair transient effects in pipeline processors is a recover strategy with variable rollback distances according to the given structural nature. According to the location and its impact to the pipeline operation, an error has to be classified in a priority group. So, the handling of multiple transient errors can be carried out according to the given priority. The difficulty is to make all possible error assumption and classify them into according priority group. As a starting point, a priority partitioning was defined according to preceding rollback strategies for a pipeline state recovery:

1. **Error(s) with a lowest priority 5 – Tolerate**
    In case of transient overwritten errors, no recovering operation is carried out.

2. **Error(s) with a low priority 4 – Micro-Rollback**
    Errors are detected within one cycle. They occurred in parts, where a simple regeneration of control-signals – respective a repetition of the last erroneous step can recover wrong data or signals.

3. **Error(s) with a middle priority 3 – Stage-Rollback**
    If a micro-rollback is no longer possible and if start-, FIFO- or 'remember'-registers of a pipeline-stage are not yet overwritten from previous stage, a restart from stage-begin and the repetition of according cycles is sufficiently.

4. **Error(s) with high priority 2 – Macro-Rollback (Pipeline-refill)**
    If a stage-rollback is impossible due to 'lost' start-registers in any stage or due to error(s) in according components itself, the execution over every – in the pipeline existing – instruction must be repeated. Therefor, the pipeline has to be refilled – starting with the furthest processed instruction (exclusive NOP).

5. Error(s) with highest priority 1 – Program repetition
In the case of occurred errors in stored program-counters, the processor has to be reset. The program must be restarted. A solution could be the implementation of checkpointing (snapshots) in order to reduce the rollback-distance.

So far, error assumptions and handling strategies are oriented on errors caused by transient effects. As outlined for the master-trailer-scheme, hot standby-hardware is needed for replacement of components with permanent faults (e.g., physical defect). A pipelined trailer is not implicitly necessary. Redundancies can be implemented according to the error-places. A permanent control-signal error does not require a replacement of the whole processor, but may be repaired with a second control-logic. Especially for safety-critical applications, a performance degradation may be acceptable. The essential requirement is to keep the functionality. A cheaper variant only with a compromise in speed could be a slave processor with a similar instruction-set but without pipelining. (The performance degradation amounts here by a factor of nearly 5 according to the pipeline depth). The complexity for data-paths may be downsized at the expense of precision. Due to these sanctions, an overhead for a trailer-processor of less than the half of the pipelined master can be expected.

5.3.2   Implementations and Results

The investigations and proposed solutions are implemented and validated with the help of a 32-bit and a 64-bit DLX-pipeline processor with single – respectively double precision and basic hazard-control [77]. A special benefit associated with distributed on-line check units, the localization of a faulty pipeline-stage or a stage-component is possible. Due to the partitioned control-signal prediction, an accurate assignment can be carried out, where a fault event has caused a processor-error. A current implementation [77] deals with control-signal-differences of two diverse control-logic-blocks. Therefore, an error classification can be carried out according to its priority and an efficient recovery by micro-RB is possible even at the fault-location. The basic architecture is outlined in Fig. 55. A more detailed description is given in [78] and shortly in the appendix.

The micro rollback for the register-file (which is here assigned to ID) is implemented according to the approach by Tamir and Trembley in [74]. For the extensive EXE-stage, different strategies are investigated according to detected errors: For register-errors, the already described register-enhancement is implemented. Errors in multiplexers, multiplier, ALU or FPU can either be handled with repetition of the full EXE-phase (stage rollback), or it can be taken advantage of the structure of multi-step FPUs or multipliers, which are commonly built with several levels. For instance, it is possible to implement control-sequences which allow to keep data of according 'interstice-registers' between FPU-levels until the next level has executed a correct operation.

The recorder-buffer of processor control-logic needs also an enhancement for rollback. Because of its job to observe start- and finish-signals of every stage, as well as the control of the whole pipe of the processor, it is very error-critical. For reasons of safety, it was decided to duplicate the whole recorder-buffer (see also Fig. 56).

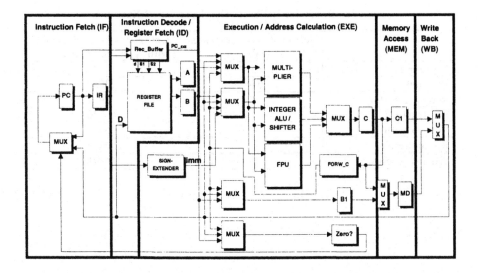

Fig. 55. Basic Pipeline Architecture of Demonstration Processor

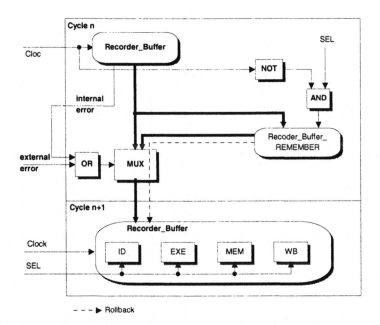

Fig. 56. DLX-Recorder Buffer with RB-Facilities

The following results were obtained for the 64-bit processor DLX64fpu_p with the implemented architecture with rollback facilities (except BISC-units).

Table 16. 'Design for Rollback' Overhead for DLX64fpu_p

	Gate count for components of the basic design	Gate count for components with *design-for-rollback*
Register-File	16537	19227
Data-path	68433	73052
Recorder buffer	1355	2911
PC structure	298	386
Control-path	4067	5579
RB-controller		2117
Whole processor(= 100%)	**72509** (= 111.4%)	**80748**

6. Conclusion and Outlook

By now, technology development in IC test has a focus on off-line test. The test process after chip – respective wafer production is more and more intolerable from the financial and time point of view. In recent time, a trend is recognizably: the partial or full migration of test technology from off-chip to on-chip. The intention is to decrease of test time and costs by a combination of on-chip and external test (particularly for SOCs). Due to improved technologies, more silicon real estate becomes less a cost problem. It could and it is used for additional test facilities (e.g. test for embedded RAM). This offers also new possibilities for on-line testing or concurrent checking. The demand for on-line techniques exists partially in today's integrated systems – especially with a safety critical relevance. For future systems with 'nano-technology', voltage levels below 1V, and clock-frequencies of several GHz, the necessity will arise for on-line check and also for fast error handling techniques. The reason will be the large part of errors caused by (today for the most part unimportant) transient effects, which cannot be handled anymore with reasonable costs.

This thesis summarizes investigations and experiments on on-line observation respective concurrent checking of processors as an useful extension to other test/check strategies. As for detection techniques, there is a distinction between component and control-signal error detection techniques. The goal was to detect single and/or multiple errors within the same clock cycle of occurrence.

The necessity for a data-path – respective data-path component observation is often doubted with the argument that a slight impreciseness of the result cannot cause a system failure. This is correct for cases, where e.g., "only one pixel is wrong". But even for memory address or offset calculation, saved pointers, etc., latent or effective data errors may have a direct impact on the system behavior.

Resting upon long research activities and experiences in on-line testing/checking, this thesis proposed refined and further-developed techniques for data-path observation.

Based on an approach for an observation of an ALU by Berger code prediction (BCP), the principle was extended to observe complete data-path structures. For relatively small register-files, the extension by additional registers for according original-register Berger code is a good solution to detect unidirectional errors. The advantage of using code registers is the detection of latent errors as well. For large register-files and bit-widths over 32-bit, the hardware overhead grows up to an unacceptable level. A higher power-consumption may be one consequence.

Beyond integer data-paths, the applicability for more complex data-paths with floating-point units was shown with the help of single- and double-precision add/sub-FPUs. Therefore, prediction formulas were developed, which consider the operation in multi-stage units. Fault-injection experiments have shown a good error detection capability. Errors at special lines are not detectable in some special operand-

ing structure in case of a transient error. But this techniques fail in the case of permanent errors. Therefore, a double-processor architecture was investigated. The master-trailer structure turns out to be a suitable solution for small processors. The trailer is delayed for one cycle. With this plus on-line checked master, a fast repair (2 cycles) of transient errors can be executed by a backup of all master-register by their counterparts in the trailer. The advantage is the function-takeover (3 cycles) in the case of a permanent-error occurrence. Based on the fact that in safety-critical systems (at minimum) a double processor is used to work fault-secure, a second processor can also be implemented as a trailer. Transient and regular non-recurring errors can be repaired without a switch to an 'emergency' mode (e.g. an electronic car-break control switches to only-mechanical control). According to the demanded grade of dependability, the trailer can also be equipped with self-checking facilities. A bi-directional register-backup is suitable for the master-trailer structure. In the case of errors within the trailer, the following scenario can be carried out, the master stops the program execution. Trailer-registers are overwritten with master-register contents with the next rising clock edge. If both processors are stable again, the master continues its operation. The trailer waits one cycle more in order to execute a one-cycle delayed operation.

The obvious problem with critical paths in backup-lines can be solved by a 'fused' implementation of both processors. A conjoint synthesis may lead to optimal results. There is nothing to be said against the placement of a trailer-register in the direct 'chip-neighborhood' of the according master-register.

For pipeline processors, the rollback technique must consider on one hand dynamical execution lengths for different stages, and on the other hand different error weightings. Therefore, a priority control was proposed to manage different rollback-actions (necessary rollback distances) for the recovery of the pipeline. An one-cycle micro-rollback, a pipeline stage-rollback, and a macro-rollback by re-filling the whole pipeline are possible. For the worst case (lost all stored return points), a program re-execution is realized. Here, the classical roll-back principle with regular checkpointing seems useful.

So far, transient errors in the pipeline are repairable with this strategies. For permanent errors (e.g. physical defects), redundant structures (e.g. backup processor) are inevitable. If a performance degradation in execution time is acceptable, a sequential standby processor is an effective solution to continue operation of the faulty pipeline processor. Because of non-pipelined execution of instruction, this processor can be designed with much less hardware. An accepted performance degradation with respect to the data precision can be realized by replacing of FPUs by simpler-precision FPUs or integer units. This may lead on one hand to smaller gate counts for the datapath of the standby processor and on the other hand to a faster execution.

So far, methods were presented to detect component and control-signal errors within the same clock cycle. Potentials for a diagnosis were explained for proposed techniques. Further investigation could improve these features for a detailed error localization. Furthermore, strategies were presented for the repair of transient faults. For the recovery in case of a permanent error, redundant structures are proposed like trailer- or backup-processors. In the case of e.g., a physical defect within the master, they take over the complete functionality. But there is an open question and a chal-

driven reduction (ADR) of additional logic can decrease the overhead. An implementation of an additional (reduced) control-logic is conceivably in order to observe a pinpointed (safety-critical) program part. The disadvantage of ADR is obviously its impact into existing (perfect) designs (e.g. 'well-designed' time-behavior). Irrespective of the unsuitability for IP-cores, the implementation of (additional) ADR-controllers has to be carried out in the actual design process. At this time, the later application is rarely known. Also, such an architecture would be inflexible because of the fixing at a defined instruction sub-set. A possible solution for this problem could be an adopted compiler, which supports only the 'defined' sub-set.

To detect control-signal errors, a basic approach may be the observation of the processor state machine, because every sequential circuit can be reduced to this abstract description. Single states and transitions could be encoded for an observation strategy. The problem is given with the complexity of combinations of simultaneous 'processor activities' (parallel operations). The question is, how these activities can be abstract. As a definitive representation of a current processor activity, active control-signals can be considered. The possibilities for control-signal combinations may be really high already for relatively simple processors. For sequential processors, they are limited to the instruction set (micro-instruction set), but possible transitions would go beyond the scope of a reasonable observation technique. In pipeline processors, the state-space 'proliferates' due to combination-possibilities of instructions, which are simultaneous within the pipeline. An observation in super-scalar- or VLIW-architectures seems to be no more manageable because of the so called 'state-space explosion'.

With the prerequisite of an access to all control-signals and the neglect of transitions, a combinatorial observation is possible. In every cycle, a number of defined control-signals is active. These signals can be encoded to a state-code, which represents the current (legal) state of the processor. If the access to control-signal conditions (instruction-, time-, flag-variables) is possible, a controller-independent generation (prediction) of the same code is realizable. A difference of a comparison of both can represent an illegal state-code. To manage more complex state machines, an application-driven reduced state-encoder or a state-space partitioning was proposed. Especially for pipeline structures, a partitioned observation of states is recommended. The principle of 'architecture-driven adoption' of state observation is applicable for all processor-architectures with a high grade of parallelism. Furthermore, a partitioning of check-units and assignment to structure-parts serves a better localization of errors.

As a consequence of a successful error detection within the same clock cycle, a fast recovery of the processor state has to be realized. The goal, especial for safety-critical applications, is obviously to use the fastest way to repair an error. Starting from the positive oriented assumption that an error has a transient character, a fast repetition of erroneous cycle(s) should deliver correct results. Classical roll-back techniques operate with 'check-pointing' or 'snap-shots'. With saved processor states in regular time-intervals, a return to a defined point is possible in an error case. Time-intervals respective rollback distances of many thousands of cycles can not satisfy demands for safety-critical (or also real time) applications. Therefore, a shorter time for recovery was implemented by micro-rollback strategies. Recent approaches to micro-rollback have rollback distances of only several machine cycles. They can recover the accord-

The overall approach for efficient on-line check and fast recover techniques enhances processor availability and improves the dependability of an embedded system at very reasonable additional costs.

lenge for further research activities: What happens with the erroneous master processor? Future research activities should investigate following assumptions: 1. The error is already localized (at least narrowed down) by diagnosis capabilities of on-line observation units. 2. The erroneous behavior of the master processor has to be analyzed. An additional on-chip test-processor can run a previously ROM-stored test-program (with legal op-codes). With the observation respective the analysis, the detection of erroneous components should be possible. This test-processor can also carry out an off-line test partitioned according to several logic and sequential components. In a recent investigation at the CE department at the BTU Cottbus a test-processor was developed, which is able to generate pseudo-random test-patterns by an integrated and programmable LFSR/MISR. Furthermore, an extensive interface is implemented in order to initiate test-programs, to put out test-patterns (serial or parallel), to read test-responses (serial or parallel), and to compare (test-)vectors. This processor needs only a gate count of approximately 3000 gates. With the assumption that the error is finally localized, the next challenge is the method of repair. 'Cold-standby' components are possible. Another possibility is given with programmable on-chip resources. They can be used to replace erroneous hardware. Within the development of the proprietary test-processor, the capability was investigated to re-program a CPLD. It can be easily adopted to other constraints for programmable logic.

A processor which is equipped with this error-detection and self-repairing features, could be used, for instance, for an embedded controller of a long term working space-probe.

A further interesting research field is a scheme with two ore more embedded processors (e.g. in a SOC). Every processor is equipped with features of an embedded test-processor. During the operation or in according time windows, these processors test each other mutually or alternately.

For an easy application of proposed and future methods, the generation of additional features should be included into design-flow of processors or processor components. A design-automation for check- and recovery-features guarantees a widespread use in real designs. The sources for observation units are basically available as generic VHDL-files. For instance, the following scenarios are imaginable. To equip a design with the cross-parity observation, the user can select according registers. The observation logic is added and will be analyzed according to its timing behavior. The tool proposes partitioning if necessary. Or, a basic processor design will be investigated automatically for rollback potentials. Necessary changes in the design structure are recommended to the designer. He defines maximum rollback-distances according to application constraints. The rollback-(priority) controller will be generated as a hardware description, which can be synthesized.

Proposed on-line error detection and fast recover techniques should be supplemented to other methods. In combination with other on-line observation principles and/or with a combined hardware-software (self-)test, these techniques are used to fulfill a complete self-check scheme for an embedded processor. Strategies for a static or dynamic (micro-) rollback are useful solutions for processor errors with transient faults of non-recurring characteristic. So, an executed program can be continued as fast as the implemented structure allows.

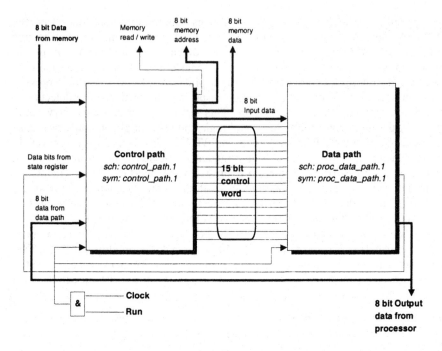

Fig. 57. Top-hierarchy view of the t4008

The DP contains an arithmetic-logical-unit (ALU) for common integer operations. The combinatorial shifter serves to carry out simple shift and rotate operations. A register-file with seven registers represents basic processor-registers. The flag-register is used for conditional instructions and 'rotate with carry' operations. Input- and output-ports are directly connected to CP.

Appendix – Demonstration Processors

To validate the suitability of proposed on-line BISC-units and the micro rollback principle, different example processors were designed. The attention was focussed on COTS-processors. Designs should represent characteristics of embedded processor-cores in various applications. In order to cover a widespread similarity with real architectures, exemplary designs are redesigns – respective derivatives of microprocessors, micro-controller CPU-cores and digital signal-processors. The following sections of this appendix should give a short overview of used processors.

Circuits were in most cases designed in a mixed manner: logic-, RTL-design and synthesized VHDL-descriptions. As design environments, Viewlogic's WorkviewOffice – respective Innoveda's Electronic Design Center and SYNOPSYS hardware-compiler were mainly and CADENCE was partly used. Designs are available as schematic, EDIF-netlist or structural VHDL-description.

A.1 Microprocessor t4008

As an example for a simple 8-bit microprocessor class, the core t4008 was implemented. The top hierarchy of the design is built with the control- (CP) and the data-path (DP). As a "von-Neumann" architecture, the CP reads instructions and data from memory and controls the DP with the control-word CW.

constellations. These errors influence the (partial) predicted Berger code, but not the real result (e.g. most significant carry- or borrow-bit). But with a minimum effort in hardware at the gate level, these signals can be generated to be fault-tolerant.

The approach on an exemplary FPU has shown that an adoption of BCP to computer arithmetic circuits with other precision scales or other architectures is feasible. Specific additional features beyond according standards can be easy included in prediction formulas (e.g. different kinds of rounding for floating-point operations). The error detection coverage can be improved by partitioning of observation circuits. A separated observation of floating-point parts (sign, biased exponent, mantissa) as well as different prediction logic for every stage are recommended.

It was outlined that the observation of processor registers or register-files may need a large number of BC-registers. Especially for large register-files, respectively for register-files with bit-widths from 32-bit upwards, the Berger code observation can not be suitable because of the amount of additional registers. As an alternative, the well-investigated observation technique by simple parity-prediction can be used. The cross-parity observation technique is a further variant, in contrary to single-parity with improved capabilities for error detection. By checking of row-, column-, and diagonal-parities, single and multiple register errors can be detected (with explained limitations). The necessary register overhead for parity vectors is much lower than for BC-registers for more complex structures. Concerning a component observation of the whole processor, the cross-parity observation is applicable to control registers (respective registers in the control-path). They can also be collected to a 'pseudo'-register-file.

The very likely impact in the timing behavior due to critical paths in the cross-parity observation logic can be extenuated by a partitioned observation of according registers. A chip can be divided according to design constraints or register locations into several rasters. Smaller observation logic and cross-parity vectors are accountable for a special chip area. Then, the error localization capability may also be improved.

Cross-parity vectors have a potentially diagnosis capability. The analysis of 'detect'-signals within the cross-parity vectors should be continued. A classification of different single and multiple error structures seems to be possible in regular register-files.

Contrary to data-path structures (data-path components), the critical character of the processor control-logic with according control-signals or the controller is commonly recognized. In a processor, various control-signals are active in parallel to control the memory access, data-path-, as well as control-path-components. Already simple errors can cause a complete failure of the processor and the whole system. Due to multi-form architectures of controllers, a general scheme is hard to find for a fast control-signal error detection technique. The easiest way is the fault-secure controller-implementation, for instance by a duplicated control-logic. With divers designs, arbitrary control-word errors should be detectable. The identification of control-word differences can be used for further recover strategies, because the target of erroneous control-signal is known. It is practicable for an error-weighting respectively a priority control. A triplicated structure can guarantee a fault-tolerant generation of control-signals until the first permanent error. For small processors, it is a practical solution. In many cases, this redundancy is not inevitably necessary. Especially in embedded systems with standard CISCs and a limited number of applications, an application-

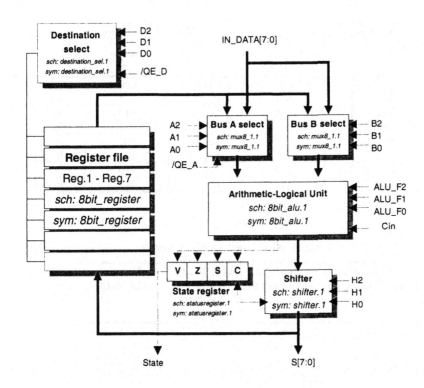

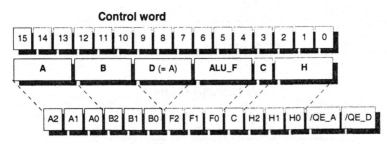

Fig. 58. Data-Path and Control-word Definition

Table 17. Destination Select

D[2:0] CW bits 9|8|7	load reg.
000	-
001	Reg. 1
010	Reg. 2
011	Reg. 3
100	Reg. 4
101	Reg. 5
110	Reg. 6
111	Reg. 7

Table 18. Source Select Signals

A_sel[2:0] CW bits 15|14|13	ALU A- INPUT	B_sel[2:0] CW bits 15|14|13	ALU B- INPUT
000	IN_DATA	000	IN_DATA
001	Reg. 1	001	Reg. 1
010	Reg. 2	010	Reg. 2
011	Reg. 3	011	Reg. 3
100	Reg. 4	100	Reg. 4
101	Reg. 5	101	Reg. 5
110	Reg. 6	110	Reg. 6
111	Reg. 7	111	Reg. 7

Table 19. ALU Function Select Signals

ALU_F[2:0], Cin CW bits 6|5|4|3	Function ALU output	ALU_F[2:0], Cin CW bits 6|5|4|3	Function ALU output
0000	F = A	100X	F = A OR B
0001	F = A+1	101X	F = A XOR B
0010	F = A+B	110X	F = A AND B
0011	F = A+B+1	111X	F = NOT A
0100	F = A-B-1		
0101	F = A-B		
0110	F = A-1		
0111	F = A; C←1		

Table 20. Shifter Control

Shifter control CW bits 2|1|0	function
000	transfer
001	Shift right
010	Shift left
011	Clear data
100	-
101	Rotate right
110	Rotate left
111	Clear data

The CP contains control- and buffer-registers. A hardwired control-logic generates control-signals and the CW for the DP according micro-instructions. An instruction flow of this *sequential* processor starts always with the fetch phase: The initialized program-counter PC is loaded into the memory-address register MAR. It addresses the first instruction within the memory. In the next cycle, the memory-buffer register

MBR is loaded with the first instruction-op-code. I will be moved to instruction-register IR, where the decoder generates the instruction variable for control-logic. After instruction decoding, different time-signal-controlled micro-instruction flows can be started.

The instruction set covers 61 instructions $(\iota_0, \iota_1, \ldots, \iota_{60})$ which are addressed with a 6-bit op-code (00_H to $3F_H$). The processor was specified as a *three-address-machine*, that means:

Destination register (A) $\leftarrow$ Source register 1 (D) <operation> Source register 2 (B)

For a reduction of the effort for addressing, a *pseudo-two-address-mode* was introduced: Destination register A is equal to Source register D. The consequence of this mode is similar to the operation of processors with an accumulator.

The addressing is organized as follow:

with A=D:
Destination register (A) $\leftarrow$ Source register(A) <operation> Source register(B)

This method needs an adaptation of the available move-instructions <MVIN x>, <MOV x y>, <MVX x> und <MVM x m>. Because the ALU can execute a data transfer without operation (A$\leftarrow$A) only at bus-port A, the destination register must also be A. In order to realize a transfer to an other register, instead of an ALU-operation *transfer* A (F=011, C=1 or F=000, C=0), an operation *addition* of B and blocked A (bus-select = disable $\rightarrow$ all A-ALU-Inputs = 0) is executed: A $\leftarrow$ 0 + B = A $\leftarrow$ B.

In the DP, there are seven processor registers are available. They are addressable with 3-bit variables A and B (control-bits 15 to 10 at bus-selectors A and B; CW-bits 9, 8, 7 = D).

Table 21. t4008 Register addresses

000	Register INP or OUT
001	Register 1 (or a)
010	Register 2 (or b)
011	Register 3 (or c)
100	Register 4 (or d)
101	Register 5 (or e)
110	Register 6 (or f)
111	Register 7 (or g)

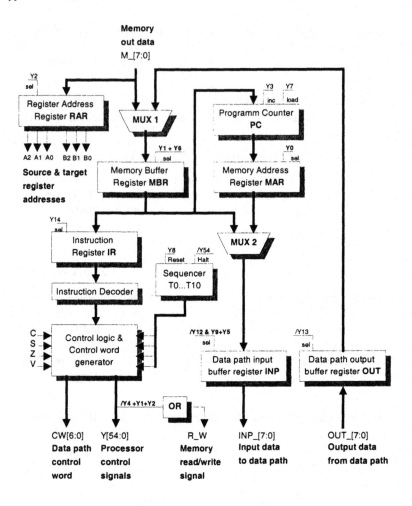

Fig. 59. Control Path of t4008

With the currently used 8-bit MAR a space of 256 memory cells is addressable. The memory width is 8-bit. For every instruction-'block' (*opcode+operand*), 3 bytes are provided.

The following figure illustrates the used instruction format:

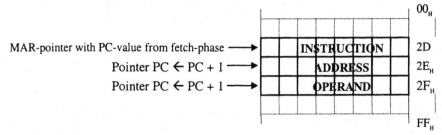

Format of instruction-block bytes:

1. INSTRUCTION-Byte

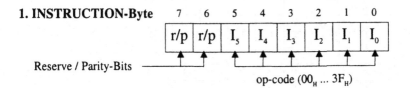

Reserve / Parity-Bits

op-code (00_H ... $3F_H$)

2. Address-Byte

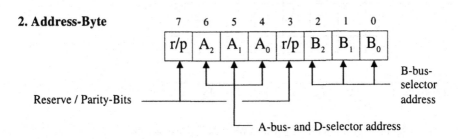

B-bus-selector address

Reserve / Parity-Bits

A-bus- and D-selector address

3. Operand

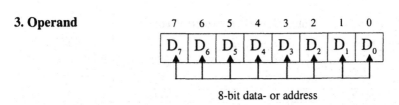

8-bit data- or address

Example 1: Two stored 8-bit numbers should be added . The result should be written back to the memory. (start address = $2D_H$):

```
JMP g 2d     # rescue old address in register 7 (=g) and jump to 2dH
MVX a 2f     # write data at 2fH to register 1
MVX b 32     # write data at 32H to register 2
ADD a b      # add a and b, write result to a
MVM a 14     # write a to memory cell 14H
RET g        # return to address[g]
```

The binary code in the memory is as follows:

◄——— Start address = 00_H

JMP	x	x	1	1	0	0	0	0
g	x	1	1	1	x	0	0	0
2d	0	0	1	0	1	1	0	1
...	...	...	...	...	...	...	...	...

◄——— Jump address = $2d_H$

MVX	x	x	0	0	0	0	1	0
a	x	0	0	1	x	0	0	0
2f	0	1	0	1	1	1	0	1

MVX	x	x	0	0	0	0	1	0
b	x	0	1	0	x	0	0	0
32	1	0	1	0	0	0	1	0
ADD	x	x	0	0	1	0	0	0
a b	x	0	0	1	x	0	1	0
	x	x	x	X	x	x	x	x
MVM	x	x	0	0	0	0	1	1
a	x	0	0	0	x	0	0	1
14	0	0	0	1	0	1	0	0
RET	x	x	1	1	0	1	1	1
g	x	0	0	0	x	1	1	1
	x	x	x	X	x	x	x	x

...   .

◄────── Result at 14_H

result	1	1	1	1	1	1	1	1

The following table contains the instruction set of processor t4008:

Table 22. t4008 Instruction Set

	Mnemonic	Format	Register transfer	$I_5 ... I_0$	A_2	A_1	A_0	B_2	B_1	B_0
00	MVIN x	x = a,b,c,d,e,f,g	Rx ← Input-Port	000000	A	A	A	x	x	x
01	MOV x y	x,y=a,b,c,d,e,f,g	Rx ← Ry	000001	A	A	A	B	B	B
02	MVX x m	x=a,b,...,g; m=XX$_H$	Rx ← M	000010	A	A	A	0	0	0
03	MVM x m	x=a,b,...,g; m=XX$_H$	M ← Rx	000011	0	0	0	B	B	B
04	INCX x	x=a,b,...,g	Rx ← Rx+1	000100	A	A	A	x	x	x
05	INCM m	m=XX$_H$	M ← M+1	000101	0	0	0	x	x	x
06	DECX x	x=a,b,...,g	Rx ← Rx-1	000110	A	A	A	x	x	x
07	DECM m	m=XX$_H$	M ← M-1	000111	0	0	0	x	x	x
08	ADD x y	x,y=a,b,c,d,e,f,g	Rx ← Rx+Ry	001000	A	A	A	B	B	B
09	ADX x m	x=a,b,...,g; m=XX$_H$	Rx ← Rx+M	001001	A	A	A	0	0	0
0A	ADM x m	x=a,b,...,g; m=XX$_H$	M ← M+Rx	001010	0	0	0	B	B	B
0B	ADC x y	x,y=a,b,c,d,e,f,g	Rx ← Rx+Ry+C	001011	A	A	A	B	B	B
0C	ACX x m	x=a,b,...,g; m=XX$_H$	Rx ← Rx+M+C	001100	A	A	A	0	0	0
0D	ACM x m	x=a,b,...,g; m=XX$_H$	M ← M+Rx+C	001101	0	0	0	B	B	B
0E	SUB x y	x,y=a,b,c,d,e,f,g	Rx ← Rx-Ry	001110	A	A	A	B	B	B
0F	SUX x m	x=a,b,...,g; m=XX$_H$	Rx ← Rx-M	001111	A	A	A	0	0	0
10	SUM x m	x=a,b,...,g; m=XX$_H$	M ← M-Rx	010000	0	0	0	B	B	B
11	SBB x y	x,y=a,b,c,d,e,f,g	Rx ← Rx-Ry-1	010001	A	A	A	B	B	B
12	SBX x m	x=a,b,...,g; m=XX$_H$	Rx ← Rx-M-1	010010	A	A	A	0	0	0
13	SBM x m	x=a,b,...,g; m=XX$_H$	M ← M-Rx-1	010011	0	0	0	B	B	B
14	not used			010100						
15	not used			010101						
16	AND x y	x,y=a,b,c,d,e,f,g	Rx ← Rx ∧ Ry	010110	A	A	A	B	B	B
17	ANX x m	x=a,b,...,g; m=XX$_H$	Rx ← Rx ∧ M	010111	A	A	A	0	0	0
18	ANM x m	x=a,b,...,g; m=XX$_H$	M ← M ∧ Rx	011000	0	0	0	B	B	B
19	OR x y	x,y=a,b,c,d,e,f,g	Rx ← Rx ∨ Ry	011001	A	A	A	B	B	B
1A	ORX x m	x=a,b,...,g; m=XX$_H$	Rx ← Rx ∨ M	011010	A	A	A	0	0	0
1B	ORM x m	x=a,b,...,g; m=XX$_H$	M ← M ∨ Rx	011011	0	0	0	B	B	B
1C	XOR x y	x,y=a,b,c,d,e,f,g	Rx ← Rx ⊕ Ry	011100	A	A	A	B	B	B

Table 22. (continued)

1D	XOX x m	x=a,b,...,g; m=XX$_H$	Rx ← Rx ⊕ M	011101	A	A	A	0	0	0
1E	XOM x m	x=a,b,...,g; m=XX$_H$	M ← M ⊕ Rx	011110	0	0	0	B	B	B
1F	CMP x y	x,y=a,b,c,d,e,f,g	Z ← 1 if (x=y), C ← 1 if (x>y)	011111	A	A	A	B	B	B
20	CPX x m	x=a,b,...,g; m=XX$_H$	Z ← 0 if (x≠y), C ← 0 if (x<y)	100000	A	A	A	0	0	0
21	CPM x m	x=a,b,...,g; m=XX$_H$	dito	100001	0	0	0	B	B	B
22	SHRX x	x=a,b,...,g	shift-right Rx, R$_7$ ← 0	100010	A	A	A	x	x	x
23	SHRM m	m=XX$_H$	shift-right Mx, M$_7$ ← 0	100011	0	0	0	x	x	x
24	SHLX x	x=a,b,...,g	shift-left Rx, R$_0$ ← 0	100100	A	A	A	x	x	x
25	SHLM m	m=XX$_H$	shift-left M, M$_0$ ← 0	100101	0	0	0	x	x	x
26	CRCX x	x=a,b,...,g	circulate right with carry	100110	A	A	A	x	x	x
27	CRCM m	m=XX$_H$	circulate right with carry	100111	0	0	0	x	x	x
28	CLCX x	x=a,b,...,g	circulate left with carry	101000	A	A	A	x	x	x
29	CLCM m	m=XX$_H$	circulate left with carry	101001	0	0	0	x	x	x
2A	CMLX x	x=a,b,...,g	Rx ← Rx'	101010	A	A	A	x	x	x
2B	CMLM m	m=XX$_H$	M ← M'	101011	0	0	0	x	x	x
2C	SETC		C ← 1	101100	0	0	0	x	x	x
2D	CLR x	x=a,b,...,g	Rx ← 0	101101	A	A	A	x	x	x
2E	CLM m			101110	0	0	0	x	x	x
2F	CLC		C ← 0	101111	0	0	0	x	x	x
30	JMP x m	x=a,b,...,g; m=XX$_H$	Rx ← PC, PC ← new adr [m]	110000	A	A	A	0	0	0
31	JNZ x m	x=a,b,...,g; m=XX$_H$	dito if Z=0	110001	A	A	A	0	0	0
32	JZ x m	x=a,b,...,g; m=XX$_H$	dito if Z=1	110010	A	A	A	0	0	0
33	JNC x m	x=a,b,...,g; m=XX$_H$	dito if C=0	110011	A	A	A	0	0	0
34	JC x m	x=a,b,...,g; m=XX$_H$	dito if C=1	110100	A	A	A	0	0	0
35	JP x m	x=a,b,...,g; m=XX$_H$	dito if S=0	110101	A	A	A	0	0	0
36	JM x m	x=a,b,...,g; m=XX$_H$	dito if S=1	110110	A	A	A	0	0	0
37	RET x	x=a,b,...,g	PC ← adr [stored in Rx]	110111	0	0	0	B	B	B
38	RNZ x	x=a,b,...,g	PC ← adr [stored in Rx] if Z=0	111000	0	0	0	B	B	B
39	RZ x	x=a,b,...,g	PC ← adr [stored in Rx] if Z=1	111001	0	0	0	B	B	B
3A	RNC x	x=a,b,...,g	PC ← adr [stored in Rx] C=0	111010	0	0	0	B	B	B
3B	RC x	x=a,b,...,g	PC ← adr [stored in Rx] C=1	111011	0	0	0	B	B	B
3C	RP x	x=a,b,...,g	PC ← adr [stored in Rx] if S=0	111100	0	0	0	B	B	B
3D	RM x	x=a,b,...,g	PC ← adr [stored in Rx] S=1	111101	0	0	0	B	B	B
3E	not used			111110						
3F	NOP		no operation	111111	x	x	x	x	x	x

A.2 Microprocessors t5008/16/32x

Processors t5008x, t5016x and t5032x represent a common instruction set similar to Intel's 8085/86, Motorola's 68000 and so one. All instruction sets base on a dynamic instruction length. The last number in the name represents the according bit range for operands. Processors named with a letter **m**, contain a fast multiplier. For instance, t5016m has a fast 8x8-bit multiplier. Letter **p** represents a pipelined instruction execution. The basic architecture is similar for all t50xx-designs. For explanation of this processor type, the t5016m is considered as a representative design.

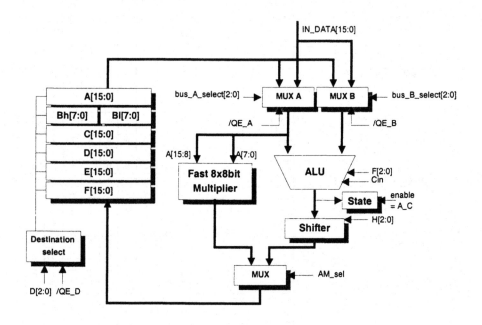

Fig. 60. t5016m Data-Path Block Diagram

The top-level contains also the data- and control-path as well as a RAM macro. The data-path is similar to the previous t4008-processor. The B-register is partitioned into two registers half of the bit length of 16-bit in order to support 8-bit operations or to swap high and low byte.

Table 23. Bus Multiplexer Control

/QE_A/B	bus_A/B_ select[2:0]	MUXA/B- out
0	XXX	0
1	000	IN[15:0]
1	001	A[15:0]
1	010	B[15:0]
1	011	B[15:0]
1	100	C[15:0]
1	101	D[15:0]
1	110	E[15:0]
1	111	F[15:0]

Table 24. Destination Select Signals

/QE_D	D[2:0]	write register
1	XXX	0
0	000	0
0	001	register A
0	010	register BH
0	011	register BL
0	100	register C
0	101	register D
0	110	register E
0	111	register F

Operands can be pass the integer ALU or the (fast) 8x8-bit multiplier. The multiplier is able to multiply the high byte with the low byte of a register content. Next tables define the control of multiplexers MUX A, MUX B and destination selector for the register-file. The control-path structure can be derived from Fig. 15. In contrast to t4008, it contains a stack-pointer SP to rescue processor state, in case of a branching.

Instructions are implicit and support immediate data, absolute and indirect addressing. The following figure outlines the implemented instruction format. The format includes one byte length for implicit instruction, two bytes for instructions with immediate 8-bit data and three bytes for instructions with 16-bit data or address.

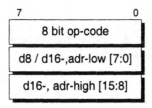

Fig. 61. t5016-Instruction Format

The memory is organized as follow: In the current implementation, a 64k area of an 8-bit RAM can be addressed. The Stack memory – addressed with stack-pointer SP – is included in a reserved area.

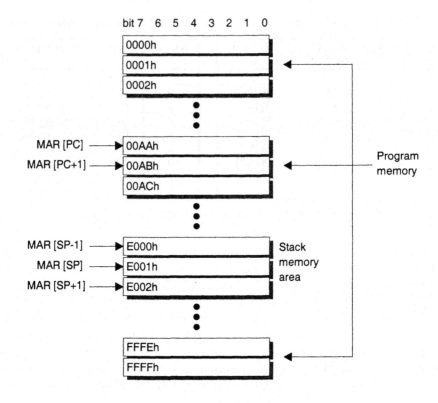

Fig. 62. t5016-Memory Organization

Following examples outline the basics of micro-operations and according register transfers. First, the fetch-phase is illustrated:

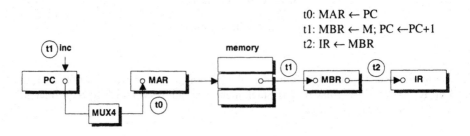

Fig. 63. t5016-Instruction Fetch Phase

The instruction **MOV B,A** needs the following data-path control signals:

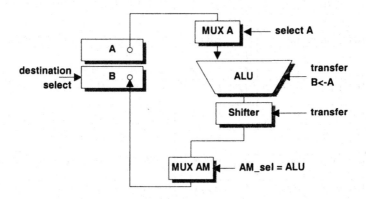

Fig. 64. t5016-Control Signals for the Execution of MOV B,A

The following table lists the complete instruction set of the t5016m microprocessor.

Table 25. t5016m – Instruction Set

Op-code			Mnemonic	Function
Hex	Binary	Instr. variable		
41	0100 0001	q65	MVM A	move register A to the memory cell with address in BH,BL
42	0100 0010	q66	MVM BH	move register BH to the memory cell with address in BH,BL
43	0100 0011	q67	MVM BL	move register BL to the memory cell with address in BH,BL
44	0100 0100	q68	MVM C	move register C to the memory cell with address in BH,BL
45	0100 0101	q69	MVM D	move register D to the memory cell with address in BH,BL
46	0100 0110	q70	MVM E	move register E to the memory cell with address in BH,BL
47	0100 0111	q71	MVM F	move register F to the memory cell with address in BH,BL
48	0100 1000	q72	MVX A	load mem-cell M (8-bit) (address BH,BL) to the register A
49	0100 1001	q73	MOV A,A	register transfer from A to A
4A	0100 1010	q74	MOV A,B	register transfer from B to A
4C	0100 1100	q76	MOV A,C	register transfer from C to A
4D	0100 1101	q77	MOV A,D	register transfer from D to A
4E	0100 1110	q78	MOV A,E	register transfer from E to A
4F	0100 1111	q79	MOV A,F	register transfer from F to A
50	0101 0000	q80	MVX BH	load mem-cell M (8-bit) (address BH,BL) to the register BH

Table 25. (continued)

51	0101 0001	q81	MOV BH,A	transf. register A high-byte (A[15:8]) to BH
54	0101 0100	q84	MOV BH,C	transf. register C high-byte (C[15:8]) to BH
55	0101 0101	q85	MOV BH,D	transf. register D high-byte (DA[15:8]) to BH
56	0101 0110	q86	MOV BH,E	transf. register E high-byte (E[15:8]) to BH
57	0101 0111	q87	MOV BH,F	transf. register F high-byte (F[15:8]) to BH
58	0101 1000	q88	MVX BL	load mem-cell M (8-bit) (address BH,BL) to the register BL
59	0101 1001	q89	MOV BL,A	transfer of the register A low-byte (A[7:0]) to BL
5C	0101 1100	q92	MOV BL,C	transfer of the register C low-byte (C[7:0]) to BL
5D	0101 1101	q93	MOV BL,D	transfer of the register D low-byte (D[7:0]) to BL
5E	0101 1110	q94	MOV BL,E	transfer of the register E low-byte (E[7:0]) to BL
5F	0101 1111	q95	MOV BL,F	transfer of the register F low-byte (F[7:0]) to BL
60	0110 0000	q96	MVX C	load mem-cell M (8-bit) (address BH,BL) to the register C
61	0110 0001	q97	MOV C,A	register transfer from A to C
62	0110 0010	q98	MOV C,B	register transfer from B to C
64	0110 0100	q100	MOV C,C	register transfer from C to C
65	0110 0101	q101	MOV C,D	register transfer from D to C
66	0110 0110	q102	MOV C,E	register transfer from E to C
67	0110 0111	q103	MOV C,F	register transfer from F to C
68	0110 1000	q104	MVX D	load mem-cell M (8-bit) (address BH,BL) to the register D
69	0110 1001	q105	MOV D,A	register transfer from A to D
6A	0110 1010	q106	MOV D,B	register transfer from B to D
6C	0110 1100	q108	MOV D,C	register transfer from C to D
6D	0110 1101	q109	MOV D,D	register transfer from D to D
6E	0110 1110	q110	MOV D,E	register transfer from E to D
6F	0110 1111	q111	MOV D,F	register transfer from F to D
70	0111 0000	q112	MVX E	load mem-cell M (8-bit) (address BH,BL) to the register E
71	0111 0001	q113	MOV E,A	register transfer from A to E
72	0111 0010	q114	MOV E,B	register transfer from B to E
74	0111 0100	q116	MOV E,C	register transfer from C to E
75	0111 0101	q117	MOV E,D	register transfer from D to E
76	0111 0110	q118	MOV E,E	register transfer from E to E
77	0111 0111	q119	MOV E,F	register transfer from F to E
78	0111 1000	q120	MVX F	load mem-cell M (8-bit) (address BH,BL) to the register F
79	0111 1001	q121	MOV F,A	register transfer from A to F
7A	0111 1010	q122	MOV F,B	register transfer from B to F
7C	0111 1100	q124	MOV F,C	register transfer from C to F
7D	0111 1101	q125	MOV F,D	Register transfer from D to F
7E	0111 1110	q126	MOV F,E	Register transfer from E to F

Table 25. (continued)

7F	0111 1111	q127	**MOV F,F**	register transfer from F to F
10	0001 0000	q16	**MVI BH,d8**	2 Byte – move directly a 8 bit-data (d8) to BH
18	0001 1000	q24	**MVI BL,d8**	2 Byte – move directly a 8 bit-data (d8) to BL
08	0000 1000	q8	**LXI A,d16**	3 Byte – move directly a 16 bit-data (d16) to register A
20	0010 0000	q32	**LXI C,d16**	3 Byte – move directly a 16 bit-data (d16) to register C
28	0010 1000	q40	**LXI D,d16**	3 Byte – move directly a 16 bit-data (d16) to register D
30	0011 0000	q48	**LXI E,d16**	3 Byte – move directly a 16 bit-data (d16) to register E
38	0011 1000	q56	**LXI F,d16**	3 Byte – move directly a 16 bit-data (d16) to register F
12	0001 0010	q18	**LDBH adr**	3 Byte – load data with address (adr) directly to BH
1A	0001 1010	q26	**LDBL adr**	3 Byte – load data with address (adr) directly to BL
01	0000 0001	q1	**STA adr**	3 Byte – store reg. A in the memory cell M with address (adr)
02	0000 0010	q2	**STBH adr**	3 Byte – store reg. BH in the memory cell with address (adr)
03	0000 0011	q3	**STBL adr**	3 Byte – store reg. BL in the memory cell with address (adr)
04	0000 0100	q4	**STC adr**	3 Byte – store reg. C in the memory cell M with address (adr)
05	0000 0101	q5	**STD adr**	3 Byte – store reg. D in the memory cell M with address (adr)
06	0000 0110	q6	**STE adr**	3 Byte – store reg. E in the memory cell M with address (adr)
07	0000 0111	q7	**STF adr**	3 Byte – store reg. F in the memory cell M with address (adr)
19	0001 1001	q25	**LDAX A**	load memory cell with address in A directly to register A
21	0010 0001	q33	**LDAX B**	load memory cell with address in B directly to register A
22	0010 0010	q34	**LDAX C**	load memory cell with address in C directly to register A
23	0010 0011	q35	**LDAX D**	load memory cell with address in D directly to register A
26	0010 0110	q38	**LDAX E**	load memory cell with address in E directly to register A
27	0010 0111	q39	**LDAX F**	load memory cell with address in F directly to register A
D1	1101 0001	q209	**PUSH A**	transfer A-content to the stack (SP-1=A-low; SP-2=A-high)
D5	1101 0101	q213	**PUSH B**	transfer B-content to the stack (SP-1=B-low; SP-2=B-high)
CF	1100 1111	q207	**PUSH C**	transfer C-content to the stack (SP-1=C-low; SP-2=C-high)
D3	1101 0011	q211	**PUSH D**	transfer D-content to the stack (SP-1=D-low; SP-2=D-high)
D9	1101 1001	q217	**PUSH E**	transfer E-content to the stack (SP-1=E-low; SP-2=E-high)
DF	1101 1111	q223	**PUSH F**	transfer F-content to the stack (SP-1=F-low; SP-2=F-high)

Table 25. (continued)

31	0011 0001	q49	POP A	transfer stack-content to A (SP=high-byte; SP+1=low-byte)
32	0011 0010	q50	POP B	transfer stack-content to B (SP=high-byte; SP+1=low-byte)
33	0011 0011	q51	POP C	transfer stack-content to C (SP=high-byte; SP+1=low-byte)
36	0011 0110	q54	POP D	transfer stack-content to D (SP=high-byte; SP+1=low-byte)
39	0011 1001	q57	POP E	transfer stack-content to E (SP=high-byte; SP+1=low-byte)
3F	0011 1111	q63	POP F	transfer stack-content to F (SP=high-byte; SP+1=low-byte)
DB	1101 1011	q219	INP A	write input-port data into register A
09	0000 1001	q9	INP B	write input-port data into register B
0A	0000 1010	q10	INP C	write input-port data into register C
0B	0000 1011	q11	INP D	write input-port data into register D
0E	0000 1110	q14	INP E	write input-port data into register E
0F	0000 1111	q15	INP F	write input-port data into register F
DD	1101 1101	q221	OUT A	put data from A register to the output-port
13	0001 0011	q19	OUT B	put data from B register to the output-port
14	0001 0100	q20	OUT C	put data from C register to the output-port
15	0001 0101	q21	OUT D	put data from D register to the output-port
16	0001 0110	q22	OUT E	put data from E register to the output-port
17	0001 0111	q23	OUT F	put data from F register to the output-port
80	1000 0000	q128	ADD M	add A with M [BH,BL] and transfer sum to A
81	1000 0001	q129	ADD A	add A with A and transfer the sum to A
82	1000 0010	q130	ADD B	add B with A and transfer the sum to A
84	1000 0100	q132	ADD C	add C with A and transfer the sum to A
85	1000 0101	q133	ADD D	add D with A and transfer the sum to A
86	1000 0110	q134	ADD E	add E with A and transfer the sum to A
87	1000 0111	q135	ADD F	add F with A and transfer the sum to A
83	1000 0011	q131	ADI d16	3 Byte – add a 16-bit-data (d16) to A and transfer the sum to register A
88	1000 1000	Q136	ADC M	add A with M[BH,BL] plus carry and transfer the sum to register A
89	1000 1001	Q137	ADC A	add A with A plus carry and transfer the sum to register A
8A	1000 1010	Q138	ADC B	add B with A plus carry and transfer the sum to register A
8C	1000 1100	q140	ADC C	add C with A plus carry and transfer the sum to register A
8D	1000 1101	q141	ADC D	add D with A plus carry and transfer the sum to register A
8E	1000 1110	q142	ADC E	add E with A plus carry and transfer the sum to register A
8F	1000 1111	q143	ADC F	Add F with A plus carry and transfer the sum to register A
DE	1101 1110	q222	ACI d16	3 Byte – add data (d16) to A plus carry; transfer the sum to register A
90	1001 0000	q144	SUB M	subtract A–M[BH,BL] and transfer the difference to register A

Table 25. (continued)

91	1001 0001	q145	SUB A	subtract A–A and transfer the difference to A
92	1001 0010	q146	SUB B	subtract A–B and transfer the difference to A
94	1001 0100	q148	SUB C	subtract A–C and transfer the difference to A
95	1001 0101	q149	SUB D	subtract A–D and transfer the difference to A
96	1001 0110	q150	SUB E	subtract A–E and transfer the difference to A
97	1001 0111	q151	SUB F	subtract A–F and transfer the difference to A
D6	1101 0110	q214	SUI d16	3 Byte – subtract A – d16 and transfer the difference to register A
98	1001 1000	q152	SBB M	subtr. A – M[BH,BL] – borrow-bit; transfer the difference to register A
99	1001 1001	q153	SBB A	subtract A – A – borrow-bit; transfer the the difference to register A
9A	1001 1010	q154	SBB B	subtract A – B – borrow-bit; transfer the difference to register A
9C	1001 1100	q156	SBB C	subtract A – C – borrow-bit; transfer the difference to register A
9D	1001 1101	q157	SBB D	subtract A – D – borrow-bit; transfer the difference to register A
9E	1001 1110	q158	SBB E	subtract A – E – borrow-bit; transfer the difference to register A
9F	1001 1111	q159	SBB F	subtract A – F – borrow-bit; transfer the difference to register A
F1	1111 0001	q241	SBI d16	3 Byte – Subtr. A – d16 – borrow-bit; transfer the difference to register A
11	0001 0001	q17	INR M	increment memory cell M with address in register [BH, BL]
0C	0000 1100	q12	INR A	increment register A
24	0010 0100	q36	INR C	increment register C
2C	0010 1100	q44	INR D	increment register D
34	0011 0100	q52	INR E	increment register E
3C	0011 1100	q60	INR F	increment register F
29	0010 1001	q41	DCR M	decrement memory cell M with address in [BH, BL]
0D	0000 1101	q13	DCR A	decrement memory cell M with address A
25	0010 0101	q37	DCR C	decrement memory cell M with address C
2D	0010 1101	q45	DCR D	decrement memory cell M with address D
35	0011 0101	q53	DCR E	decrement memory cell M with address E
3D	0011 1101	q61	DCR F	decrement memory cell M with address F
E0	1110 0000	q224	MUL M	load A with the product high-byte · low-byte of M[BH, BL]
E1	1110 0001	q225	MUL A	load A with the product high-byte · low-byte of A
E2	1110 0010	q226	MUL B	load A with the product high-byte · low-byte of B
E4	1110 0100	q228	MUL C	load A with the product high-byte · low-byte of C
E5	1110 0101	q229	MUL D	load A with the product high-byte · low-byte of D
E6	1110 0110	q230	MUL E	load A with the product high-byte · low-byte of E

Table 25. (continued)

E7	1110 0111	q231	**MUL F**	load A with the product high-byte · low-byte of F
E8	1110 1000	q232	**MIBH d8**	2 Byte – load A with the product (BH · d8); (BL will be lost)
E9	1110 1001	q233	**MIBL d8**	2 Byte – load A with the product (BL · d8); (BH will be lost)
EA	1110 1010	q234	**MUX**	3 Byte – Multiplication d16[15:8] · d16[7:0]; transfer to A
A0	1010 0000	q160	**ANA M**	load A with result from high- AND low-Byte of M[BH, BL]
A1	1010 0001	q161	**ANA A**	load A with the result from A AND A
A2	1010 0010	q162	**ANA B**	load A with the result from A AND B
A4	1010 0100	q164	**ANA C**	load A with the result from A AND C
A5	1010 0101	q165	**ANA D**	load A with the result from A AND D
A6	1010 0110	q166	**ANA E**	load A with the result from A AND E
A7	1010 0111	q167	**ANA F**	load A with the result from A AND F
C7	1100 0111	q199	**ANI d16**	3 Byte - load A with result from d16 AND A
B0	1011 0000	q176	**ORA M**	load A with the result from high- OR low-byte of M[BH, BL]
B1	1011 0001	q177	**ORA A**	load A with the result from A OR A
B2	1011 0010	q178	**ORA B**	load A with the result from A OR B
B4	1011 0100	q180	**ORA C**	load A with the result from A OR C
B5	1011 0101	q181	**ORA D**	load A with the result from A OR D
B6	1011 0110	q182	**ORA E**	load A with the result from A OR E
B7	1011 0111	q183	**ORA F**	load A with the result from A OR F
F6	1111 0110	q246	**ORI d16**	3 Byte – load A with result from d16 OR A
A8	1010 1000	q168	**XRA M**	load A with the result from high- XOR low-byte of M[BH, BL]
A9	1010 1001	q169	**XRA A**	load A with the result from A XOR A
AA	1010 1010	q170	**XRA B**	load A with the result from A XOR B
AC	1010 1100	q172	**XRA C**	load A with the result from A XOR C
AD	1010 1101	q173	**XRA D**	load A with the result from A XOR D
AE	1010 1110	q174	**XRA E**	load A with the result from A XOR E
AF	1010 1111	q175	**XRA F**	load A with the result from A XOR F
3E	0011 1110	q62	**XRI d16**	3 Byte – load A with result from d16 XOR A
3A	0011 1010	q58	**RLC**	rotate the accumulator A left circular
3B	0011 1011	q59	**RRC**	rotate the accumulator A right circular
2F	0010 1111	q47	**CMA**	load A with the complement of A
37	0011 0111	q55	**SEC**	set the carry-Flag
B8	1011 1000	q184	**CPI d16**	3 Byte – compare A with immediate data d16
B9	1011 1001	q185	**CMP M**	compare A with memory the cell M[BH, BL] and set flags
BA	1011 1010	q186	**CMP A**	compare A with A and set flags
BB	1011 1011	q187	**CMP B**	compare A with B and set flags
BC	1011 1100	q188	**CMP C**	compare A with C and set flags
BD	1011 1101	q189	**CMP D**	compare A with D and set flags
BE	1011 1110	q190	**CMP E**	compare A with E and set flags

Table 25. (continued)

BF	1011 1111	q191	**CMP F**	compare A with F and set flags
C3	1100 0011	q195	**JMP adr**	3 Byte – jump unconditionally to the memory address (adr)
C2	1100 0010	q194	**JNZ adr**	3 Byte – jump to adress if Zero-flag = 0
CA	1100 1010	q202	**JZ adr**	3 Byte – jump to adress if Zero-flag = 1
D2	1101 0010	q210	**JNC adr**	3 Byte – jump to adress if Carry-flag = 0
DA	1101 1010	q218	**JC adr**	3 Byte – jump to adress if Carry-flag = 1
F2	1111 0010	q242	**JP adr**	3 Byte – jump to adress if Sign-flag = 0
FA	1111 1010	q250	**JM adr**	3 Byte – jump to adress if Sign-flag = 1
CD	1100 1101	q205	**CALL adr**	3 Byte – routine call at adr, rescue actual address to the Stack
C4	1100 0100	q196	**CNZ adr**	3 Byte – routine call if Z=0, rescue actual address to the Stack
CC	1100 1100	q204	**CZ adr**	3 Byte – routine call if Z=1, rescue actual address to the Stack
D4	1101 0100	q212	**CNC adr**	3 Byte – routine call if C=0, rescue actual address to the Stack
DC	1101 1100	q220	**CC adr**	3 Byte – routine call if C=1, rescue actual address to the Stack
F4	1111 0100	q244	**CP adr**	3 Byte – routine call if S=0, rescue actual address to the Stack
FC	1111 1100	q252	**CM adr**	3 Byte – routine call if S=1, rescue actual address to the Stack
C9	1100 1001	q201	**RET**	3 Byte – return to the rescued address stored to the Stack
C0	1100 0000	q192	**RNZ**	3 Byte – return to the rescued address stored to the Stack if Z=0
C8	1100 1000	q200	**RZ**	3 Byte – return to the rescued address stored to the Stack if Z=1
D0	1101 0000	q208	**RNC**	3 Byte – return to the rescued addr. stored to the Stack if C=0
D8	1101 1000	q216	**RC**	3 Byte – return to the rescued addr. stored to the Stack if C=1
F0	1111 0000	q240	**RP**	3 Byte – return to the rescued addr. stored to the Stack if S=0
F8	1111 1000	q248	**RM**	3 Byte – return to the rescued addr. stored to the Stack if S=1
00	0000 0000	q0	**NOP**	no operation – program pause
1B	0001 1011	q27	**LXSP d16**	load stack pointer with immediate–data (d16)
1C	0001 1100	q28	**LDSP**	load stack pointer with data from register B

A.3 Digital Signal Processors uDSP32a/b

Processors uDSP32a and uDSP32b are universal digital signal processors with a data processing bit-width of 32-bit. The structure of the version 'a' is similar to the architecture of the t5032 to process 32-bit integer data. The 32-bit instruction format (bits [31:24] = op-code; bits [23:0] = data memory address) is oriented to the Harvard-principle: The memory space for instructions and data are separately addressable. Therefor, the control-path consists of two memory address registers. Special instructions are implemented in order to load or store double data or six data words in order to support faster data processing. DSP version uDSP32b consists of single pre-cision floating point addition, subtraction, and multiplication.

Table 26. Micro -Operations of the Fetch-Phase

Mnemonic	$q_x t_x$	Control Signals	Micro-operations	Function
Fetch	$q_x t_0$	y_0	IMAR ← PC	instruction and
	$q_x t_1$	y_1, y_2, y_3	IMBR ← IM, PC ← PC + 1, DMAR ← IM	operand fetch
	$q_x t_2$	y_4, y_{10}	IR ← IMBR, READBUFFER ← INP	

Table 27. Single-Data Load/Store Instruction

Mnemonic	$q_x t_x$	Control signal	Micro-Operation	Function
LD A,addr	$q_1 t_3$	y_{13}	A ← READBUFFER	load data at address
	$q_1 t_4$	y_9	T ← 0	to register A
LD B,addr	$q_2 t_3$	y_{14}	B ← READBUFFER	load data at address
	$q_2 t_4$	y_9	T ← 0	to register B
LD C,addr	$q_3 t_3$	y_{15}	C ← READBUFFER	load data at address
	$q_3 t_4$	y_9	T ← 0	to register C
LD D,addr	$q_4 t_3$	y_{16}	D ← READBUFFER	load data at address
	$q_4 t_4$	y_9	T ← 0	to register D
LD E,addr	$q_5 t_3$	y_{17}	E ← READBUFFER	load data at address
	$q_5 t_4$	y_9	T ← 0	to register E
LD F,addr	$q_6 t_3$	y_{18}	F ← READBUFFER	load data at address to register F
ST addr,A	$q_7 t_3$	y_{11}, y_{19}	WRITEBUFFER ← A	store register A to
	$q_7 t_4$	y_{12}	OUT ← WRITEBUFFER	memory (address)
	$q_7 t_5$	y_9	T ← 0	
ST addr,B	$q_8 t_3$	y_{11}, y_{20}	WRITEBUFFER ← B	store register B to
	$q_8 t_4$	y_{12}	OUT ← WRITEBUFFER	memory (address)
	$q_8 t_4$	y_9	T ← 0	
ST addr,C	$q_9 t_3$	y_{11}, y_{21}	WRITEBUFFER ← C	store register C to
	$q_9 t_4$	y_{12}	OUT ← WRITEBUFFER	memory (address)
	$q_9 t_4$	y_9	T ← 0	
ST addr,D	$q_{10} t_3$	y_{11}, y_{22}	WRITEBUFFER ← D	store register D to
	$q_{10} t_4$	y_{12}	OUT ← WRITEBUFFER	memory (address)
	$q_{10} t_4$	y_9	T ← 0	
ST addr,E	$q_{11} t_3$	y_{11}, y_{23}	WRITEBUFFER ← E	store register E to
	$q_{11} t_4$	y_{12}	OUT ← WRITEBUFFER	memory (address)
	$q_{11} t_4$	y_9	T ← 0	
ST addr,F	$q_{12} t_3$	y_{11}, y_{24}	WRITEBUFFER ← F	store register F to
	$q_{12} t_4$	y_{12}	OUT ← WRITEBUFFER	memory (address)
	$q_{12} t_4$	y_9	T ← 0	

Table 28. Double-Data Load/Store Instruction

Mnemonic	$q_x t_x$	Control Signal	Micro-Operation	Function
LDB AB,addr	$q_{13}t_3$	$Y_{13},\ Y_6$	A ← READBUFFER, DMAR ← DMAR + 1	load two data words to register A and B
	$q_{13}t_4$	Y_{10}	READBUFFER ← INP	
	$q_{13}t_5$	Y_{14}	B ← READBUFFER	
	$q_{13}t_6$	Y_9	T ← 0	
LDB CD,addr	$q_{14}t_3$	$Y_{15},\ Y_6$	C ← READBUFFER, DMAR ← DMAR + 1	load two data words to register C and D
	$q_{14}t_4$	Y_{10}	READBUFFER ← INP	
	$q_{14}t_5$	Y_{16}	D ← READBUFFER	
	$q_{14}t_6$	Y_9	T ← 0	
LDB EF,addr	$q_{15}t_3$	$Y_{17},\ Y_6$	E ← READBUFFER, DMAR ← DMAR + 1	load two data words to register E and F
STB addr,AB	$q_{16}t_3$	$Y_{11},\ Y_{19}$	WRITEBUFFER ← A	store register A and B to the memory (address)
	$q_{16}t_4$	Y_{12}	OUT ← WRITEBUFFER	
	$q_{16}t_5$	$Y_{11},\ Y_{20},\ Y_6$	WRITEBUFFER ← B, DMAR ← DMAR + 1	
	$q_{16}t_6$	Y_{12}	OUT ← WRITEBUFFER	
	$q_{16}t_7$	Y_9	T ← 0	
STB addr,CD	$q_{17}t_3$	$Y_{11},\ Y_{21}$	WRITEBUFFER ← C	store register C and D to the memory (address)
	$q_{17}t_4$	Y_{12}	OUT ← WRITEBUFFER	
	$q_{17}t_5$	$Y_{11},\ Y_{22},\ Y_6$	WRITEBUFFER ← D, DMAR ← DMAR + 1	
	$q_{17}t_6$	Y_{12}	OUT ← WRITEBUFFER	
	$q_{17}t_7$	Y_9	T ← 0	
STB addr,EF	$q_{18}t_3$	$Y_{11},\ Y_{23}$	WRITEBUFFER ← E	store register E and F to the memory (address)
	$q_{18}t_4$	Y_{12}	OUT ← WRITEBUFFER	
	$q_{18}t_5$	$Y_{11},\ Y_{24},\ Y_6$	WRITEBUFFER ← F, DMAR ← DMAR + 1	
	$q_{18}t_6$	Y_{12}	OUT ← WRITEBUFFER	
	$q_{18}t_7$	Y_9	T ← 0	

Table 29. Six Data Word Load Instruction

Mnemonic	$q_x t_x$	Control Signal	Micro-Operation	Function
LOADALL addr	$q_{46}t_3$	$Y_{13},\ Y_6$	A ← READBUFFER, DMAR ← DMAR + 1	load six data words to register A to F
	$q_{46}t_4$	Y_{10}	READBUFFER ← INP	
	$q_{46}t_5$	$Y_{14},\ Y_6$	B ← READBUFFER, DMAR ← DMAR + 1	
	$q_{46}t_6$	Y_{10}	READBUFFER ← INP	
	$q_{46}t_7$	$Y_{15},\ Y_6$	C ← READBUFFER, DMAR ← DMAR + 1	
	$q_{46}t_8$	Y_{10}	READBUFFER ← INP	
	$Q_{46}t_9$	$Y_{16},\ Y_6$	D ← READBUFFER, DMAR ← DMAR + 1	

Table 29. (continued)

$q_{46}t_{10}$	Y_{10}	READBUFFER ← INP	
$q_{46}t_{11}$	Y_{17}, Y_6	E ← READBUFFER, DMAR ← DMAR + 1	
$q_{46}t_{12}$	Y_{10}	READBUFFER ← INP	
$q_{46}t_{13}$	Y_{18}	F ← READBUFFER	
$q_{46}t_{14}$	Y_9	T ← 0	

Table 30. Move Instruction

Mnemonic	$q_x t_x$	Control Signal	Micro-Operation	Function
MOV A,F	$q_{19}t_3$	Y_{25}	A ← F	move A to F
	$q_{19}t_4$	Y_9	T ← 0	
MOV B,F	$q_{20}t_3$	Y_{26}	B ← F	move B to F
	$q_{20}t_4$	Y_9	T ← 0	
MOV C,F	$q_{21}t_3$	Y_{27}	C ← F	move C to F
	$q_{21}t_4$	Y_9	T ← 0	
MOV D,F	$q_{22}t_3$	Y_{28}	D ← F	move D to F
	$q_{22}t_4$	Y_9	T ← 0	
MOV E,F	$q_{23}t_3$	Y_{29}	E ← F	move E to F
	$q_{23}t_4$	Y_9	T ← 0	
MOV F,B	$q_{24}t_3$	Y_{30}	F ← B	move F to B
	$q_{24}t_4$	Y_9	T ← 0	
MOV F,C	$q_{25}t_3$	Y_{31}	F ← C	move F to C
	$q_{25}t_4$	Y_9	T ← 0	
MOV F,D	$q_{26}t_3$	Y_{32}	F ← D	move F to D
	$q_{26}t_4$	Y_9	T ← 0	
MOV F,E	$q_{27}t_3$	Y_{33}	F ← E	move F to E
	$q_{27}t_4$	Y_9	T ← 0	

Table 31. Integer Instruction

Mnemonic	$q_x t_x$	Control signal	Micro-Operation	Function
INC A	$q_{28}t_3$	Y_{34}	A ← A + 1	increment A
	$q_{28}t_4$	Y_9	T ← 0	
INC B	$q_{29}t_3$	Y_{35}	B ← B + 1	increment B
	$q_{29}t_4$	Y_9	T ← 0	
DEC A	$q_{30}t_3$	Y_{36}	A ← A - 1	decrement A
	$q_{30}t_4$	Y_9	T ← 0	
DEC B	$q_{31}t_3$	Y_{37}	B ← B - 1	decrement B
	$q_{31}t_4$	Y_9	T ← 0	
CPL A	$q_{32}t_3$	Y_{38}	A ← ¬A	complement A
	$q_{32}t_4$	Y_9	T ← 0	
CPL B	$q_{33}t_3$	Y_{39}	B ← ¬B	complement B
	$q_{33}t_4$	Y_9	T ← 0	
ADD A,B	$q_{34}t_3$	Y_{40}	A ← A + B	add A and B and trans-fer the sum to A
	$q_{34}t_4$	Y_9	T ← 0	

Table 31. (continued)

ADDC A, B	$q_{35}t_3$ $q_{35}t_4$	Y_{41} Y_9	A ← A + B + 1 T ← 0	add A and B + Carry and transfer sum to A
SUB A,B	$q_{36}t_3$ $q_{36}t_4$	Y_{42} Y_9	A ← A - B T ← 0	subtract A - B and transfer difference to A
SUBB A,B	$q_{37}t_3$ $q_{37}t_4$	Y_{43} Y_9	A ← A - B - 1 T ← 0	subtract A - B – bor- row, transfer difference to A
OR A,B	$q_{40}t_3$ $q_{40}t_4$	Y_{46} Y_9	A ← A ∨ B T ← 0	load A with A OR B
EXOR A,B	$q_{41}t_3$ $q_{41}t_4$	Y_{47} Y_9	A ← A ⊕ B T ← 0	load A with A XOR B
AND A,B	$q_{42}t_3$ $q_{42}t_4$	Y_{48} Y_9	A ← A ∧ B T ← 0	load A with A AND B
CMP A,B	$q_{43}t_3$ $q_{43}t_4$	Y_{49} Y_9	CMP A,B (A-B) T ← 0	compare A and B
ADDI A,addr	$q_{57}t_3$ $q_{57}t_4$	Y_{53} Y_9	A ← A + addr T ← 0	add memory content (address) to register A
SUBI A,addr	$q_{58}t_3$ $q_{58}t_4$	Y_{54} Y_9	A ← A - addr T ← 0	subtract memory con- tent (address) to regis- ter A
ANDI A,addr	$q_{60}t_3$ $q_{60}t_4$	Y_{56} Y_9	A ← A ∧ addr T ← 0	register A AND mem- ory content (address)
ORI A,addr	$q_{61}t_3$ $q_{61}t_4$	Y_{57} Y_9	A ← A ∨ addr T ← 0	register A OR memory content (address)
EXORI A,addr	$q_{62}t_3$ $q_{62}t_4$	Y_{58} Y_9	A ← A ⊕ addr T ← 0	register A EXOR memory content (ad- dress)
MUL A,B	$q_{38}t_3$ $q_{38}t_4$	Y_{44} Y_9	A ← B[31:16] * B[15:0] T ← 0	load A with product of low- and high-bytes of B
MUL C,B	$q_{39}t_3$ $q_{39}t_4$	Y_{45} Y_9	C ← B[31:16] * B[15:0] T ← 0	load C with product of low- and high-Bytes of B
MULTI A,addr	$q_{59}t_3$ $q_{59}t_4$	Y_{55} Y_9	A ←addr[31:16] * addr[15:0] T ← 0	load A with product of low- and high-Bytes of memory (address)
MUL64AB addr	$q_{47}t_3$ $q_{47}t_4$ $q_{47}t_5$ $q_{47}t_6$ $q_{47}t_7$ $q_{47}t_8$	Y_{50} Y_{51}, Y_{11} Y_{12} $Y_6, Y_{52},$ Y_{11} Y_{12} Y_9	MREG64 ← A[31:0] * B[31:0] WRITEBUFFER ← REG[31 :0] OUT ← WRITEBUFFER DMAR ← DMAR + 1, WRITEBUFFER ← REG[63 :32] OUT ← WRITEBUFFER T ← 0	multiply register A and B, and write product to memory (address and address+1)

Table 32. Branch Instruction

Mnemonic	$q_x t_x$	Control signal	Micro-Operation	Function
JMP addr	$q_{44}t_3$ $q_{44}t_4$	y_5 y_9	PC ← DMAR T ← 0	jump unconditioned to address
RET addr	$q_{45}t_3$	y_5	PC ← DMAR	return unconditioned to address
JC addr	$q_{48}t_3$ $q_{48}t_4$	y_5 y_9	PC ← DMAR, if C T ← 0	jump if CARRY = 1
JNC addr	$q_{49}t_3$ $q_{49}t_4$	y_5 y_9	PC ← DMAR, if ¬C T ← 0	jump if CARRY = 0
JZ addr	$q_{50}t_3$ $q_{50}t_4$	y_5 y_9	PC ← DMAR, if Z T ← 0	jump if ZERO = 1
JNZ addr	$q_{51}t_3$ $q_{51}t_4$	y_5 y_9	PC ← DMAR, if ¬Z T ← 0	jump if ZERO = 0
JV addr	$q_{52}t_3$ $q_{52}t_4$	y_5 y_9	PC ← DMAR, if V T ← 0	jump if OVERFLOW = 1
JNV addr	$q_{53}t_3$ $q_{53}t_4$	y_5 y_9	PC ← DMAR, if ¬V T ← 0	jump if OVERFLOW = 0
JS addr	$q_{69}t_3$ $q_{69}t_4$	y_5 y_9	PC ← DMAR, if S T ← 0	jump if SIGN = 1
JNS addr	$q_{70}t_3$ $q_{70}t_4$	y_5 y_9	PC ← DMAR, if ¬S T ← 0	jump if SIGN = 0
CALL addr	$q_{54}t_3$ $q_{54}t_4$ $q_{54}t_5$ $q_{54}t_6$	y_{79} y_{79}, y_{80} y_5 y_9	STP.sel STP.sel, STP.inc PC ← DMAR T ← 0	jump and save processor state at the stack
RET	$q_{55}t_3$ $q_{55}t_4$ $q_{55}t_5$	y_{81}, y_{82} y_{83}, y_5 y_9	STR.sel, STP.dec PC.sel, PC ← DMAR T ← 0	return to address – loaded from stack

Table 33. NOP Instruction

Mnemonic	$q_x t_x$	Control Signal	Micro-operation	Function
NOP	$q_{56}t_3$	y_9	T ← 0	no operation

Table 34. Floating Point Instruction

Mnemonic	$q_x t_x$	Control Signal	Micro-Operation	Function
ADDF A, B	$q_{63}t_3$	y_{59}	A ← A + B (L1)	add float numbers in registers A and B (4 cycles), transfer result to A
	$q_{63}t_4$	y_{60}	A ← A + B (L2)	
	$q_{63}t_5$	y_{61}	A ← A + B (L3)	
	$q_{63}t_6$	y_{62}	A ← A + B (L4)	
	$q_{63}t_7$	y_{84}	A ← A + B (res)	
	$q_{63}t_8$	y_9	T ← 0	
SUBF A, B	$q_{64}t_3$	y_{63}	A ← A − B (L1)	subtract float numbers in registers A and B (4 cycles), transfer result to A
	$q_{64}t_4$	y_{64}	A ← A − B (L2)	
	$q_{65}t_5$	y_{65}	A ← A − B (L3)	
	$q_{64}t_6$	y_{66}	A ← A − B (L4)	
	$q_{64}t_7$	y_{85}	A ← A − B (res)	
	$q_{64}t_8$	y_9	T ← 0	
MULTF A, B	$q_{65}t_3$	y_{67}	A ← A * B (L1)	multiply float numbers in registers A and B (2 cycles), transfer result to A
	$q_{65}t_4$	y_{68}	A ← A * B (L2)	
	$q_{65}t_5$	y_{86}	A ← A * B (res)	
	$q_{65}t_6$	y_9	T ← 0	
ADDFI A, addr	$q_{66}t_3$	y_{69}	A ← A + addr (L1)	add float number in register A and memory (address) (4 cycles)
	$q_{66}t_4$	y_{70}	A ← A + addr (L2)	
	$q_{66}t_5$	y_{71}	A ← A + addr (L3)	
	$q_{66}t_6$	y_{72}	A ← A + addr (L4)	
	$q_{66}t_7$	y_{87}	A ← A + addr (res)	
	$q_{66}t_8$	y_9	T ← 0	
SUBFI A, addr	$q_{67}t_3$	y_{73}	A ← A − addr (L1)	subtract float number in register A and memory (address) (4 cycles)
	$q_{67}t_4$	y_{74}	A ← A − addr (L2)	
	$q_{67}t_5$	y_{75}	A ← A − addr (L3)	
	$q_{67}t_6$	y_{76}	A ← A − addr (L4)	
	$q_{67}t_7$	y_{88}	A ← A − addr (res)	
	$q_{67}t_8$	y_9	T ← 0	
MULTFI A, addr	$q_{68}t_3$	y_{77}	A ← A * addr (L1)	multiply float number in register A and memory (address) (2 cycles)
	$q_{68}t_4$	y_{78}	A ← A * addr (L2)	
	$q_{68}t_5$	y_{89}	A ← A * addr (res)	
	$q_{68}t_6$	y_9	T ← 0	

A.4 Pipeline Processors DLX32/64fpu_p

The architecture of these processors is based on a modified DLX-scheme by Hennessey and Patterson, which was described in [39]. The Harvard-architecture contains an instruction- and a data-RAM. The design is partitioned into control- (CP) and data-path (DP). The CP has a full accessibility to all control-signal. The DP contains a fast multiplier, a integer ALU and a floating point unit for single – respective double precision signed addition or subtraction (IEEE standard 754). Furthermore, the DP contains a register-file with 32 fix-point- or 16 floating-point registers (64-bit for DLX64).

The instruction-set is derived from [39]. An interrupt-handling functionality is not considered yet. The extension for this feature is easily implementable, because according lines exists (e.g. MA_ERR from FPU). Implemented instructions are listed in the following table:

Table 35. DLX32/64fpu_p Instruction Set

Instruction	Type	Meaning
ADD	Integer	Addition of two register-contents
ADDD	Floating point	Addition of two register-contents
ADDI	Integer	Addition of a register-content and an immediate
SUB	Integer	Subtraction of two register-contents
SUBD	Floating point	Subtraction of two register-contents
SUBI	Integer	Subtract an immediate from a register content
MUL	Integer	Multiplication of two register-contents
AND	Integer	AND-operation of two register-contents
ANDI	Integer	AND-operation of a register-content with an immediate
OR	Integer	OR-operation of two register-contents
ORI	Integer	OR-operation of a register-content and an immediate
XOR	Integer	Exclusive-OR-operation of two register-contents
XORI	Integer	Exclusive-OR-operation of a register-content and an immediate
SLL	Integer	One-bit logical left-shift of a register content
SRL	Integer	One-bit logical right-shift of a register content
SRA	Integer	One-bit arithmetical right-shift of a register content
J	Control	Jump PC-relative with 26-bit immediate
JR	Control	Jump register-direct
JAL	Control	Jump PC-relative with 26 bit immediate and write PC in register R31
JALR	Control	Jump register-direct and write PC in register R31
BEQZ	Control	Branch PC-relative with 16-bit immediate if register-content = zero
BNEZ	Control	Branch PC-relative with 16-bit immediate if register-content ≠ zero
LIW	Transport int.	Load least-significant 32-bit of a registers
LI	Transport int.	Load a 64-bit word of a registers
LD	Transport int.	Load a 64-bit word of a registers

Table 35. (continued)

SIW	Transport int.	Store least-significant 32-bit of a registers
SI	Transport int.	Store 64-bit of a registers
SD	Transport fp	Store 64-bit of a registers
MOVI	Transport int.	Move register content to another register
MOVD	Transport fp	Move register content to another register
NOP	Control	No operation
HALT	Control	Processor halt

Instructions of DLX32/64fpu_p processors have a static instruction length. They support register-direct, displacement and immediate address-modes. The instruction-formats are organized as follows:

I – Type-instructions

6	5	5	16
Op-code	rs1	rd	Immediate

Load and store of words and double-words
ALU-operations with Immediate (rd ← rs1 op Immediate)

Conditional branch instructions
Jump register, Jump and Link Register
(rd=0, rs1= Destination, Immediate=0)

R – Type- instructions

6	5	5	5	11
Op-code	rs1	rs2	rd	func

Register-register-ALU-operation: rd ← rs1 func rs2
Data operations: Add, Sub, etc.

J – Type- instructions

6	26
Op-code	Offset added to PC

Jump, jump and link

The pipeline processor has the following stages according Fig. 49:
1. Instruction fetch (IF)
2. Instruction decode and register fetch (ID)
3. Execution and address calculation (EXE)
4. Memory access (MEM)
5. Write back (WB)

The currently implemented duration for separate stages is organized as follows:

IF: 3 cycles
ID: 3 cycles
EXE: integer ALU, multiplier – 2cycles / FPU – 6 cycles
MEM: 6 cycles
WB: 2 cycles

Micro-instructions-sequences are outlined in the following table:

Table 36. DLX32/64fpu_p Micro-Instruction Sequences

Instr	IF	ID	EXE	MEM	WB
LIW	MAR←PC IR←M[MAR]	A←Src.1 B←Src.2	C←A+IMM	MAR2←C MD_LOW←M[MAR2]	Dest. ←MD_LOW
LI	MAR←PC IR←M[MAR]	A←Src.1 B←Src.2	C←A+IMM (integer)	MAR2←C MD_HIGH←M[MAR2] MAR←MAR+1 MD_LOW←M[MAR2]	Destination←MD
LD	MAR←PC IR←M[MAR]	A←Src.1 B←Src.2	C←A+IMM (integer)	MAR2←C MD_HIGH←M[MAR2] MAR←MAR+1 MD_LOW←M[MAR2]	Destination←MD
SIW	MAR←PC IR←M[MAR]	A←Src.1 B←Src.2	C←A+IMM (integer) B1←B	MAR2←C MD←B1 M[MAR2]←MD_LOW	
SI	MAR←PC IR←M[MAR]	A←Src.1 B←Src.2	C←A+IMM (Integer) B1←B	MAR2←C MD←B1 M[MAR2] ←MD_HIGH MAR←MAR+1 M[MAR2] ←MD_LOW	
SD	MAR←PC IR←M[MAR]	A←Src.1 B←Src.2	C←A+IMM (Integer) B1←B	MAR2←C MD←B1 M[MAR2] ←MD_HIGH MAR←MAR+1 M[MAR2] ←MD_LOW	
MOVI	MAR←PC IR←M[MAR]	A←Src.1 B←Src.2	C←A	C1←C	Destination←C1
MOVD	MAR←PC IR←M[MAR]	A←Src.1 B←Src.2	C←A	C1←C	Destination←C1
ADD	MAR←PC IR←M[MAR]	A←Src.1 B←Src.2	C←A+B (integer)	C1←C	Destination←C1
ADDD	MAR←PC IR←M[MAR]	A←Src.1 B←Src.2	C←A+B (fl. point)	C1←C	Destination←C1
ADDI	MAR←PC IR←M[MAR]	A←Src.1 B←Src.2	C←A+IMM (integer)	C1←C	Destination←C1
SUB	MAR←PC IR←M[MAR]	A←Src.1 B←Src.2	C←A-B (integer)	C1←C	Destination←C1

Table 36. (continued)

SUBD	MAR←PC IR←M[MAR]	A←Src.1 B←Src.2	C←A-B (fl. point)	C1←C	Destination←C1
SUBI	MAR←PC IR←M[MAR]	A←Src.1 B←Src.2	C←A-IMM (integer)	C1←C	Destination←C1
MUL	MAR←PC IR←M[MAR]	A←Src.1 B←Src.2	C←A*B (integer)	C1←C	Destination←C1
AND	MAR←PC IR←M[MAR]	A←Src.1 B←Src.2	C←A ∩ B (integer)	C1←C	Destination←C1
ANDI	MAR←PC IR←M[MAR]	A←Src.1 B←Src.2	C←A ∩ IMM (integer)	C1←C	Destination←C1
OR	MAR←PC IR←M[MAR]	A←Src.1 B←Src.2	C←A ∪ B (integer)	C1←C	Destination←C1
ORI	MAR←PC IR←M[MAR]	A←Src.1 B←Src.2	C←A ∪ B (integer)	C1←C	Destination←C1
XOR	MAR←PC IR←M[MAR]	A←Src.1 B←Src.2	C←A ⊕ B (integer)	C1←C	Destination←C1
XORI	MAR←PC IR←M[MAR]	A←Src.1 B←Src.2	C←A ⊕ B (integer)	C1←C	Destination←C1
SLL	MAR←PC IR←M[MAR]	A←src.1 B←Src.2	C←SLL A	C1←C	Destination←C1
SRL	MAR←PC IR←M[MAR]	A←Src.1 B←Src.2	C←SRL A	C1←C	Destination←C1
SRA	MAR←PC IR←M[MAR]	A←Src.1 B←Src.2	C←SRA A	C1←C	Destination←C1
BEQZ	MAR←PC IR←M[MAR]	A←Src.1 B←Src.2	C←PC + IMM (integer) Compare←B	PC←C if zero	
BNEZ	MAR←PC IR←M[MAR]	A←Src.1 B←Src.2	C←PC + IMM (integer) Compare←B	PC←C if not zero	
J	MAR←PC IR←M[MAR]	A←Src.1 B←Src.2	C←PC + IMM (integer)	PC←C	
JR	MAR←PC IR←M[MAR]	A←Src.1 B←Src.2	C←A (integer)	PC←C	
JAL	MAR←PC IR←M[MAR]	A←Src.1 B←Src.2	C←PC + IMM (integer) B1←PC	PC←C MD←B1	Destination←MD
JALR	MAR←PC IR←M[MAR]	A←Src.1 B←Src.2	C←A (integer) B1←PC	PC←C MD←B1	Destination←MD
NOP	MAR←PC IR←M[MAR]	A←Src.1 B←Src.2			
HALT	MAR←PC IR←M[MAR]				

Abbreviations, Symbols and Identifiers

ADR	Application driven reduction
ASIP	Application specific instruction set processor
ASP	Architecture specific partitioning
ALU	Arithmetic logic unit
BCP	Berger (code) check prediction
BIST	Built-in self-test
BISC	Built-in self-check
CISC	Complex instruction set computers
CL	Control logic
CLA	Carry-look-ahead (adder)
CMOS	Complementary MOS
COTS	Commercial of-the-shelf
CP	Control path
CPI	Clocks per instruction
CPLD	Complex programmable logic device
CPP	Cross-parity prediction
CPU	Central processing unit
CSP	Control signal prediction
CW	Control word
DP	Data path
DSP	Digital signal processor
EEPROM	Electrical erasable PROM
ENIAC	Electronic numerical integrator and calculator
FIFO	First-in first out
FT	Fault-tolerant
FS	Fault secure
FSM	Finite state machine
HDL	Hardware description language
IC	Integrated circuit
ID	Instruction decoder
IP	Intellectual property
IR	Instruction register
JTAG	Joint Test Action Group
LFSR	Left feedback shift register
MAR	Memory address register
MBR	Memory buffer register
MIMD	Multiple instruction Stream, Multiple Data Stream
MISD	Multiple instruction Stream, Single Data Stream
MISR	Multiple input shift register
μOp	Micro-operation
MOS	Metal-oxide-semiconductor (transistor)

PC	Program counter
PROM	Programmable read-only memory
RAM	Read access memory
RAPID	Reusable Application Specific Intellectual Property Developers
RISC	Reduced instruction set computers
RB	Rollback
ROM	Read-only memory
RTL	Register transfer level
Op-code	Operation code respective binary coded instruction
sa0	Stuck-at-zero (fault)
sa1	Stuck-at-one (fault)
SISD	Single instruction stream, single data stream
SIMD	Single instruction stream, multiple data stream
SOB	System-on-board
SOC	System-on-chip
SP	Stack pointer
TMR	Triple-modular redundancy
Vdd	Power supplier or logic '1'
UDL	User defined logic
VHDL	VHSIC hardware description language
VHSIC	Very high speed integrated circuit
VLIW	Very long instruction word (processor)
VSIA	Virtual Socket Interface Alliance
Vss	Ground or logic '0'

List of Figures

List of Tables

References

1. M. Abramovici, M.A. Breuer, A.D. Friedman: Digital System Testing and Testable Design, IEEE Press, New York, ISBN 0-7803-1062-4, 1990
2. K.-T. Cheng, S. Dey, M. Rodgers, K. Roy: Test Challenges for Deep Sub-Micron Technologies, DAC2000, Los Angeles (CA), pp. 142-149
3. R.K. Gupta, Y. Zorian: Introducing Core-Based System Design, IEEE Design & Test Of Computers Oct.-Dec. 1997, pp. 15-25
4. Y. Zorian, E.J. Marinissen, S. Dey: Testing Embedded-Core Based System Chips, ITC 1998, pp. 130-143
5. Y. Zorian, E.J. Marinissen: System Chip Test: How Will It Impact Your Design?, DAC2000, Los Angeles, CA
6. IEEE Computer Society: IEEE Standard Test Access Port and Boundary-Scan Architecture – IEEE Std. 1149.1-1990, IEEE, New York, 1990
7. IEEE P1500 Web Site: http://grouper.ieee.org/groups/1500
8. A.P. Ströle, H.J. Wunderlich: TESTCHIP: A Chip for Weighted Random Pattern Generation, Evaluation and Test Control, IEEE Journal of Solid State Circuits, Vol. 26, No. 7, July 1991, pp. 1056-1063
9. A. Auer, R. Kimmelmann: Schaltungstest mit Boundary Scan, Hüthig Verlag, ISBN 3-7785-2519
10. D.K. Pradhan: Fault-Tolerant Computer System Design, Prentice Hall, NJ, 1996, ISBN: 0-13-057887-8
11. U. Gläser: Mehrebenen-Testgenerierung für synchrone Schaltwerke, GMD-Bericht Nr. 235, 1994, Oldenburg-Verlag, ISBN 3-486-23193-6
12. U. Gläser, U. Hübner, H.T. Vierhaus: Mixed Level Hierarchical Test Generation for Transition Faults and Overcurrent Related Defects, Proc. International Test Conference, Baltimore, MD, USA, Sept. 1992, pp. 21-29
13. U. Gläser, H. T. Vierhaus: Mixed-Level Test Generation for Synchronous Sequential Circuits using the FOGBUSTER Algorithm, IEEE Transactions of Computer-Aided Design of ICs, Vol. 15, No, 4, April 1996, pp. 410-423
14. W. Meyer, R. Camposano: Fast Hierarchical Multi-Level Fault Simulation of Sequential Circuits with Switch-Level Accuracy, 30th ACM/IEEE DAC, 1993, p. 515 – 519
15. M. Pflanz, H.T. Vierhaus: Generating Reliable Embedded Processors, IEEE MICRO Sept./Oct. 1998, pp. 33-41
16. M. Pflanz, C. Rousselle, H.T. Vierhaus: Possibilities and Limitations of Self-Test and Functional Backup for Standard Processor Cores in Embedded Applications, European Test Workshop, May 1999, Constance, Germany
17. M. Pflanz, H.T. Vierhaus: An Efficient On-Line-Test and Recover Scheme for Embedded Processors, 10th European Workshop on Dependable Computing, May 1999, Vienna, pp. 63-69
18. M. Pflanz, F. Pompsch, H. Hennig, H.T. Vierhaus: Efficient Backup Schemes for Processors in Embedded Systems, European Material Conference (E-MRS), June 1999, Symposium M, paper M-II.3 and in Journal Solid-State Electronics, No. 44, 2000, pp. 791-796
19. M. Pflanz, F. Pompsch, H.T. Vierhaus: An Efficient On-Line-Test and Back-up Scheme for Embedded Processors, Proceedings Int. Test Conference, ITC'99, Atlantic City, MA, pp. 964-972

20. M. Pflanz, C. Galke, H.T. Vierhaus: A New Method for On-Line State Machine Observation for Embedded Microprocessors, Proc. IEEE Int. High Level Design Validation and Test Workshop, Nov. 2000, Berkeley, CA, pp. 34-39

21. M. Pflanz, K. Walther, H.T. Vierhaus: On-line Error Detection Techniques for Dependable Embedded Processors with High Complexity, Int. On-line Test Workshop (IOLTW'01), July, 2001, Taormina, Italy

22. B.W. Johnson: Design and Analysis of Fault-Tolerant Digital Systems, Addison-Wesley Publishing Company, Reading, Mass., 1989, p. 173

23. P.C.Li, T.K.Young: Electromigration: The time bomb in deep-submicron Ics, IEEE Spectrum, Sept. 1996, pp.75-78

24. K.W. Li, J.R. Armstrong, J.G. Tront: An HDL Simulation of the Effects of Single Event Upsets On microprocessor Program Flow, IEEE Trans. on Nuclear Science, Vol. NS-31, No. 6, Dec. 1984

25. M. Nicolaidis: Online Testing for VLSI: State of the Art and Trends; Integration the VLSI Journal, No. 28, 1998, pp. 197-209

26. A.Benson, M.Rebaudengo, L.Impagliazzo, P.Marmo: Fault List Collapsing for Fault Injection Experiments, Annual Reliability and Maintainability Symposium, 1998, pp.383-388

27. R.D. Eldred: Test Routines Based on Symbolic Logic Statements, Journal of the ACM, January 1959, pp. 33-36

28. R.L. Wadsack: Fault Modelling and Logic Simulation in CMOS and MOS Integrated Circuits, Bell Systems Technical Journal, May-June 1978, pp. 1449-1474

29. R.K. Gulati, G.F. Hawkins: Iddq Testing of VLSI Circuits, Kluwer Academic Publishers, Boston, 1993

30. J.M. Acken: Testing for Bridging Faults (Shorts) in CMOS Circuits, 1983 Design Automation Conference, pp. 717-718, 1983

31. K.J. Lee, M.A. Breuer: On detecting Single and Multiple Bridging Faults in CMOS Circuits Using Current Supply Monitoring Method, 1990 International Conference on Circuits and Systems, May 1990

32. T.M Storey, W. Maly: CMOS Bridging Fault Detection, 1990 International Test Conference, Sept. 1990, pp. 842-851

33. H.T. Vierhaus, W. Meyer, U. Gläser: CMOS Bridges and Resistive Transistor Faults: IDDQ versus Delay Effects, Int. Test Conference 1993, Baltimore, USA, pp. 83-91

34. P.K. Lala: Digital circuit Testing and Testability, Academic Press, ISBN 0-12-434330-9

35. M. Rimén, J. Ohlson: A Study of the Error Behavior of a 32-bit RISC Subjected to Simulated Transient Fault Injection, Proc. Of the Int. Test Conference 1992, Baltimore, USA, pp. 696-704

36. C. Rousselle: Entwicklung eines RT-/Logik-Simulators auf der Basis von hierarchischen Schaltungsbeschreibungen in VHDL, Master thesis at the CE Dept., BTU Cottbus, Germany, October 2000

37. A. Behling: Entwicklung eines minimierenden Fehlerlistengenerators, Master thesis at the CE Dept., BTU Cottbus, Germany, October 2000

38. C. Rousselle, M. Pflanz, A. Behling, T. Mohaupt, H.T. Vierhaus: A Register-Transfer-Level Fault Simulator for Permanent and Transient Faults in Embedded Processors, DATE'01, Munich, March 2001, Germany

39. D.A. Patterson, J.L. Hennessy: Computer Organization and Design – The Hardware/Software Interface; Morgan Kaufmann Publishers Inc., San Francisco, CA, 1998

40. http://ei.cs.vt.edu/~history/Zuse.html

41. M.M. Mano: Digital Logic and Computer Design, Prentice-Hall Inc., New Jersey, 1979, ISBN 0-13-214510-3

42. M.J. Flynn: Very high-speed computing systems, Proc. IEEE 54:12, Dec. 1966, pp. 396, 591

43. A. Bode: RISC-Architecturen, Reihe Informatik, Band 60, BI Wissenschaftsverlag, Mannheim, 1990, ISBN 3-411-14752-0

44. E.J. Marinissen, Y. Zorian, R. Kapur, T. Taylor, L. Whetsel: Towards a Standard for Embedded Core Test: An Example, Proc. ITC'99, Atlantic City, NJ, Oct. 1999, pp. 616-627

45. A.R. Weiss: The Standardization of Embedded Benchmarking: Pitfalls and Opportunities, Proc. IEEE Int. Conf. On Computer Design, ICCD'99, Austin, TX, Oct. 1999, pp. 492-498

46. M.F. Jacome, G. deVeciana: Design Challanges for New Application-Specific Processors, IEEE Design & Test of Computers, April-June 2000, pp. 40 - 50

47. A. Amendola, A. Benso, F. Corno, L. Impagliazzo, P. Prinetto, M. Rebaudengo, M. Sonza Reorda: Faulty Behavior Observation on a Microprocessor System through a VHDL Simulation-Based Fault Injection Experiment, IEEE EURO-VHDL'96, Geneva (Switzerland), September 1996

48. A. Benso, M. Rebaudengo, M. Sonza Reorda: Fault Injection for Embedded Microprocessor-based Systems; Journal of Universal Computer Science (Special Issue on Dependability Evaluation and Validation), 1998, Vol. 5, No. 5, pp. 693-711

49. J.A. Clark, D.K. Pradhan: Fault Injection – A Method for Validating Computer-System Dependability, IEEE Computer, June 1995, pp. 47-56

50. M. Gössel, S. Graf: Error Detection Circuits, McGraw-Hill Book Company, London, ISBN 0-07-707438-6, 1993

51. F.F. Sellers, M.J. Hsiao, L.W. Bernson: Error Detecting Logic for Digital Computers, McGraw-Hill Book Company, New York, 1968

52. R.H. Minero, A.J. Anello, R.G. Furey, L.R. Palounek: Checking by Pseudoduplication, US Patent 3660646,GO6F 11/00, 1972

53. N.T. Wing, E. Glen: Self Checking Arithmetic Unit, US Patent 4314350, GO6F 11/14

54. J.M. Berger: A Note on Error Detecting Codes for Asymmetric channels, Information and Control, vol. 4, pp 68-73, 1961

55. A. Morosow, V.V. Saposhnikov, Vl.V. Saposhnikov, M. Goessel: Self-Checking Circuits with Unidirectionally Independent Outputs Journal VLSI Design, Vol 5 No 4. pp. 333-345, 1998

56. S. Mitra, E. McCluskey: Which Concurrent Error Detection scheme to Choose?, International Test Conference, Atlantic City, NJ, USA, 2000, pp. 985-994

57. V. Otscheretnij, M. Goessel, Vl.V. Saposhnikov, V.V. Saposhnikov: Fault-Tolerant Self-dual Circuits with Error Detection by Parity- and Group Parity Prediction, Proc. 4th IEEE International On-Line Testing Workshop, pp.124-130, Capri, Italy, 1998

58. C. Zeng, N. Saxena, E.J. McCluskey: Finite State Machine Synthesis with concurrent Error Detection, Proc. ITC'99, Atlantic City, NJ, 1999, pp. 672-679

59. J-C. Lo, S. Thanawastien, T.R.N. Rao, M. Nicolaidis: An SFS Berger Check Prediction ALU and Its Application to Self-Checking Processor Designs, IEEE Trans. On CAD, Vol. 11, No. 4, April 1992, pp.525-540

60. Lattice™ Semiconductor Corporation: Macro Library Reference Manual, Version 4.00, 1996

61. R. Leveugle, T. Michel, G. Saucier: Design of Microprocessors with Built-In On-Line Test, Proc. IEEE 20th Int. Symp. On Fault-Tolerant Computing, Los Alamitos, CA, June 1990, pp. 450-456

62. M.A. Schuette, J.P. Shen: Processor Control Flow Monitoring Using Signatured Instruction Streams, IEEE Transactions on Computers, vol. C-36, No. 3, March 1987, pp. 264-275

63. G. Miremadi, J. Ohlson, M. Riemén, J. Karlsson: Use of Time and Address Signatures for Control Flow Checking, Dependable Computing for Critical Applications, No. 5, IEEE Computer Society, 1998, pp. 201-221

64. S. Hellebrand and H. Wunderlich, "An Efficient Procedure for the Synthesis of Fast Self-Testable Controller Structures," Proc. Int'l Conf. Computer-Aided Design, IEEE Computer Society Press, Los Alamitos, Calif., 1994, pp. 110-116

65. S.N. Hamilton, A. Hertwig, A. Orailoglu: Self Recovering Controller and Datapath Codesign, DATE 1999

66. E. Voskamp, W. Rosenstiel: Error Detection in Fault Secure Controllers using State Encoding, Proc. European Design & Test Conference, March 1996, Paris, pp. 200-204
67. P.K. Lala: Self-Checking and Fault-Tolerant Digital Design; Morgan Kaufmann Publishers, San Francisco, CA, 2000
68. URL = http://www.stratus.de/informationen/systemdesign.htm
69. URL = http://www.sun.com/smi/Press/sunflash/9606/sunflash.960624.4689.html
70. D.Powell, et al.Guards: a generic upgradable architecture for real-time dependable systems, LAAS-CNRS Rapport No. 98259, June 1998, Toulouse, France, 32p
71. C.F. Webb: S/390 microprocessor design, IBM Journal Res. Develop., Vol. 44, No. 6, November 2000, pp. 899-907
72. M. Rebaudengo, M. Sonza Reorda, M. Torchiano, M. Violante: Soft-error Detection through Software Fault-Tolerance techniques, IEEE International Symposium on Defect and Fault Tolerance in VLSI Systems, Nov. 1999, Albuquerque, New Mexico, USA
73. R. Koo, S. Toueg: Checkpointing and Rollback-Recovery for Distributed Systems, IEEE Trans. on Software Engineering, Vol. SE-13, January 1987, pp. 23-31
74. Y. Tamir, M. Tremblay: High-Performance Fault-Tolerant VLSI Systems Using Micro Rollback, IEEE Trans. on Computers, Vol. 39, No. 4, April 1990, pp. 548-554
75. Y.Tamir, M. Liang, T. Lai, M. Tremblay: The UCLA Mirror Processor: A Builing Block for Self-Checking Self-Repairing Computing Nodes, Proc. 21th Intl. Symposium on Fault-Tolerant Computing (FTCS), 1991, Montreal, Canada
76. M. Nicolaidis, R.O. Duarte, S. Manich, J. Figueras: Fault-Secure Parity Prediction Arithmetic Operators, IEEE Design & Test of Computers, April-June, 1997
77. C. Galke: Rollback-Strategies for Processors with a Pipeline Structure, Master-Thesis (in German) at the CE Dept., BTU Cottbus, Germany, October 2000
78. M. Pflanz: Cross-Parity-Prediction, applied for a patent at the German Patent and Trademark Office (Deutsches Patent- und Markenamt), Febr., 2001, No.: 12070181

Lecture Notes in Computer Science

For information about Vols. 1–2199
please contact your bookseller or Springer-Verlag